JESUS FOR MODERN MAN

JESUS
FOR MODERN MAN

An Introduction to the Gospels
in Today's English Version

DAVID L. EDWARDS

Sir, we want to see Jesus
John 12:21

Collins
Fontana Books

In co-operation with
The Bible Reading Fellowship

First published in Fontana 1975

© David L. Edwards 1975

Made and printed in Great Britain by
William Collins Sons & Co Ltd Glasgow

TO KATHLEEN DOWNHAM
a wonderful colleague and friend

CONTENTS

PREFACE

For years, as a result of many conversations, I have
wanted to write a book which would say simply and
clearly what we can know about the historical Jesus
and what we can begin to understand about his
teaching and achievement. Many of the books in this
field are so technical that the average reader does not
tackle them, while others are so 'popular' that they
do not rest on the honest examination of the evidence, which modern people rightly demand. Of course
there are some books which popularize scholarship in
the way I want, but rightly or wrongly I still feel that
there is room for a fresh attempt to combine an
account of the evidence with an attempt to discuss its
significance to us.

I know that my own account is unsatisfactory, and
that I have failed in my attempt. I know, too, that
some will think the position I have reached too
modernist and radical, while others will think it too
orthodox and conservative. But I am delighted to
have been given the opportunity to tell the truth as I
see it by the initiative of the publishers. This book is
based on Today's English Version, a translation of the
New Testament that has already sold millions of copies
throughout the world – although in some places, few
but important, I do not hesitate to criticize that translation, and it is certainly my hope that readers who
prefer other translations will still find this book useful.
Almost all biblical quotations are given in full. This
little book, which I hope amounts to an introduction to
the gospels, is a volume in a series introducing various

parts of Today's English Version. In that series, it is accompanied by Pierson Parker's *Good News in Matthew*, by Robert Crotty's *Good News in Mark*, by Wilf Wilkinson's *Good News in Luke*, and by Douglas Webster's *Good News in John*. It has been a privilege and delight to have been associated with Lady Collins in planning the series.

The list of books suggested for further reading acknowledges some of my debts.

D.L.E.

THE QUEST FOR TRUTH

According to Luke, Jesus said: 'I came to set the earth on fire' (12:49). We shall discuss later what Jesus of Nazareth may have meant by such words if he said them. What concerns us now is that Luke evidently did not think it a fantastic claim when he wrote, about fifty years after the death of Jesus. Obviously he was aware that there had been no world-consuming bonfire. But he was able to record that, both before and after his death, the personality of Jesus had attracted many. All of them could have used the words of the disciples in Luke's story: 'Wasn't it like a fire burning in us when he talked to us on the road?' (24:32) That was enough to keep alive the hope that the most bloodstained earth could be ignited.

The effect of Jesus has been much the same since the first Christian century. He has fascinated, and in a sense dominated, many countries in many periods. In many parts of the world he remains at the centre of the spiritual life of our age. His message may be twisted, but he is still named and thought about – with real consequences outside, as well as within, those circles which proudly accept the heritage of the Christian Church. Many who are in revolt against the Church still honour Jesus greatly. In non-Christian countries many traces of the impact of Jesus can be observed, although naturally the situation there is more open to dispute since he is seldom named. Values which in history are associated with him more than with anyone else (and which have been spread by Christianity despite the howling faults of Christians) are very widely respected

and even practised – the values of a strict purity combined with an energetic compassion in the setting of
a trust that right will prevail. The spiritual nobility of
this Jew of the first century AD is almost everywhere
admired, and the spiritual revolution which took his
name is almost everywhere welcomed. In all history no
man has had such an influence.

In a way the popularity of Jesus has created our
problem. For many people today, he is still a figure so
highly respected that he is lifted right out of contact
with everyday reality. Many who are, as they say,
'not religious' regard him as the teacher of perfect
ethics – a man so pure that the morality he taught
has little or nothing to do with the sordid world of conflicts and problems. So in effect Jesus is banished to
a golden-olden never-never land, perpetually preaching
the Sermon on the Mount while angels sing in the
background and no one really listens. And many who
are more religious seem to think that it is enough to
repeat that 'Jesus is God'. The danger is that he may
actually be the baby doll in the Nativity play, or the
fairhaired friend of the traditional Bible illustrations
(sweet but curiously soft), or the lifeless figure in the
stained glass window. So in effect the humanity of
Jesus is denied.

Sentimental pictures of Jesus are fragile. For the
popularity of Jesus is not the whole story. Almost
everywhere in the world today Jesus is under criticism,
the storm of controversy is growing, and only tough-
minded accounts of him are going to survive the
storm. Increasingly people notice those elements in
the gospels' portrait of Jesus that the sentimentalists
ignore – his urgency, his imperious demands, his terrible warnings. The character of Jesus evidently
demands honest study and honest explanation. And

what was his purpose? Some highly critical suggestions have been made by scholars over the last two centuries. These points have not been confined to scholarly circles. They are public property. They strengthen many non-Christians in their resistance to the Christian religion. They stop many parents or school-teachers teaching Christianity in Christian countries. They are points made over coffee or beer. And unless they can be answered truthfully, the influence of Jesus seems bound to diminish.

In 1774 *Fragments by an Unknown Author* began to be published in German. Eventually seven little volumes appeared. Edited by the philosopher G. E. Lessing without any author's name, they were in fact the work of H. S. Reimarus, a teacher of Oriental languages who had died in 1768. The last of these fragments was *On the Purpose of Jesus and His Disciples*. It was the beginning of the modern attempt to recover the 'true' Jesus. According to Reimarus, Jesus was a faithful Jew whose message was a simple one: the 'Messianic' kingdom – in other words, political victory for the Jews – was near. After his crucifixion his followers, who were still ambitious, stole and hid his corpse. They also invented a religion about him as the spiritual saviour of mankind.

The publication of such ideas aroused such a storm that it became all the more obvious how wise Reimarus had been to keep his thoughts to himself. Lessing, who had caused the shock by publishing this material, wrote a book on the gospels. Although it was less controversial it, too, did not appear until after its author's death. But fortunately something more than indignation followed the appearance of such provocative theories. Particularly in Germany but also in America, England, France, and elsewhere, many scholars joined the debate. A great number of Lives of Jesus appeared, technical or popular. Some of these were as destructive as Reimarus had been. Others presented an appealing Jesus by painting the portrait of a gentle poet who had loved nature and all mankind; or by depicting a preacher who was keen on social progress. It was a just comment on this kind of Life of Jesus that the author was like a man looking into a deep well and seeing at the bottom the reflection of . . . his own face. Then in 1906 Albert Schweitzer, the brilliant scholar who later became world-famous as a medical mission-ary in Africa, published a 'history of Jesus research' from Reimarus to the latest of the critics, William Wrede. This was translated into English under the arresting title, *The Quest of the Historical Jesus*.

Its main conclusions struck many readers as being two. First, the nineteenth-century Lives of Jesus were so varied in their interpretations, and depended so clearly on how their authors felt about Christianity, that it seemed impossible that any reliable biography could ever be written. Second, Schweitzer's own theories (formed some years previously but incorporated at the end of *The Quest*) seemed at least as plausible as any of the others. To Schweitzer, Jesus was the greatest of all men, a man of God with the most sublime vision, faith, and courage. Jesus believed passionately and an-nounced urgently that, in a matter of weeks, God would bring in his Kingdom. This would be not a political affair as Reimarus had thought, but a complete miracle resulting in a total change for the world. When Jesus saw that the Kingdom had not come during his mission in Galilee, his disappointment turned into the conviction that God demanded a final sacrifice: his crucifixion. When on his cross Jesus saw that still the Kingdom did not come, he died in despair.

Since Schweitzer's book of 1906 the debate about the historical Jesus has been resumed, although most scholars have agreed that the quest should not continue in the style of the nineteenth-century Lives of Jesus. Many fresh suggestions have been made. It is not too much to say that the first-century world, or what is known of it, has been ransacked in the hunt for clues.

At one time the storm-centre of the debate was the theory that Christianity first flourished as one of the many myths which grew like luxuriant weeds in the 'mystery' religions of the first century. According to this theory, although the first Christians were Jews, Christianity itself was, or rapidly became, essentially non-Jewish or 'Gentile'. Some of these Gentile myths pictured a divine revealer who descended from heaven to earth and then ascended back again. Others pictured a god who died and rose again like the earth in winter and spring. Such myths were familiar in the Greek and Egyptian cults of Serapis, Osiris, Isis, and others; and it was argued that Christianity had combined its own myth very effectively with more practical items in the Near Eastern religious world of the day – the impressive initiation ceremonies, the worshippers' club with its secrets about the god, the meal which was also communion with the god, and so forth.

This theory left unsolved the puzzle of who the Jew was whose life had been a pretext for the foundation of Christianity. Some extremists argued that he had never existed. Another line was that he had never existed as more than a fairly conventional Jewish rabbi. But since the Second World War attention has shifted from the 'mystery' religions back to the soil of Palestine and the colourful fringes of the religion of the Jews. The discovery of an amazing hoard of ancient scrolls at Qumran in the desert near the Dead Sea began in 1947. These scrolls were the records of a monastery belonging to the Essenes, a highly austere and fanatical sect which believed that it would play a vital part in the rapidly approaching end of history. The natural excitement about such a find has led many to see close similarities between the Jesus movement and the Qumran monastery.

All the radical suggestions, from Reimarus to Schweitzer and beyond, have had in common an objection to trusting the New Testament. It is not merely a question of details in the New Testament being false to the historical facts. If any of these radical ideas is true, the central message of the New Testament is thoroughly fraudulent. For example, if it is true that Jesus really was seeking a political kingdom before Pontius Pilate executed him for doing just that, the New Testament is fraudulent in saying that Jesus preached a peaceful collaboration with the Romans then occupying Palestine.

If it is true that Jesus pinned everything on the miraculous Kingdom of God coming or being made to come in the very near future, the New Testament is fraudulent in saying that the mission to the whole world is absolutely right since Jesus had disclaimed knowledge of when the Kingdom would come. In Matthew's gospel comes the verse which Albert Schweitzer said sparked off his whole theory: 'I tell you, you will not finish your work in all the towns of Israel before the Son of Man comes' (10:23). But in the same gospel we notice other verses which show what Matthew believed. 'No one knows . . . when that day and hour will come – neither the angels in heaven, nor the Son; the

Father alone knows' (24:36). 'This Good News about the Kingdom will be preached through all the world, for a witness to all mankind; and then will come the end' (24:14). 'Go . . . to all peoples everywhere . . . and remember! I will be with you always, to the end of the age' (28:19, 20). It is evident that Matthew would have been horrified by Schweitzer's reconstruction of the historical Jesus – yet Matthew is Schweitzer's key witness.

If it is true that the mystery religions shaped the whole character of Christianity, the New Testament is fraudulent in never mentioning these religions except to attack them. If it is true that Jesus was a conventional Jewish rabbi, the New Testament is fraudulent in giving so much emphasis to the conflicts between Jesus and the religion around him. And if the Essenes hold the key, the New Testament is fraudulent in not mentioning them at all.

The question now is whether any of these radical theories is necessary in order to make sense of the evidence surviving about the historical Jesus. That question cannot be answered without a careful investigation.

Some evidence survives outside the New Testament, but not much. In his *Annals* written about 115 the Roman historian Tacitus reports that the Christians in Rome were accused of setting fire to Rome under the Emperor Nero in the year 64, and he adds: 'Christus, from whom their name is derived, was condemned to death in the reign of Tiberius by the procurator Pontius Pilate'. In his short biography of the Emperor Claudius written a few years later, another Roman historian, Suetonius, says that Claudius 'banished from Rome the Jews, who were continually making a disturbance at the instigation of Chrestus'. Perhaps all that such references show is that Jesus Christ was being talked about in Rome.

Jewish writers could be expected to be far better informed about the founder of Christianity. Unfortunately, however, the earliest evidence surviving from the Jewish rabbis probably comes from a time more than forty years after the death of Jesus. It is both scrappy and hostile. It tells of a Jesus of Nazareth who practised sorcery and mocked at the words of the wise, leading Israel astray. He was the illegitimate son of a Jewish mother and had five special disciples. He was hanged on the eve of a Passover which fell on the Sabbath (Saturday). Such an account of Jesus may be mainly a reaction to Christian propaganda about his healing miracles, new teaching, virgin birth, and redeeming death – but at least it shows that the rabbis then felt unable to deny part of what the Christians asserted: a Jew called Jesus had existed as a wonder-worker and teacher with a considerable following.

It is also unfortunate that the *Jewish War* and the *Antiquities* of Flavius Josephus the Jewish historian, written within the first century, have not come down to us with any clear references to Jesus. The references that are included in the Slavonic translations were probably added to the original text by Christians (apart perhaps from a mention of James 'the brother of Jesus who was called Christ'). These references were highly respectful of this 'man – if "man" is the right word' – who 'was the Christ.' Some mystery surrounds them because they are not accurately based on the gospels in the New Testament; for example, it is said of Jesus that he was 'to be found mainly in the Mount of Olives', and that he gathered round him '150 assistants and masses of followers', and that Pilate at first released him because Jesus had healed his wife – until the Jews bribed him with 'thirty talents'. Although there is this maddening uncertainty at the central point in his evidence, Josephus does give us an unforgettable picture of the sordid brutality of the régime of the Herods, the fanatical Jewish revolt, and the Roman campaign which crushed it. Josephus himself deserted the cause of the rebellion when he was captured by the Romans, and lived comfortably in Rome under imperial patronage. His personal references to religion are all somewhat vague, although he defended the Jewish faith against attacks. He describes the same Palestine as the gospels do, and yet . . .

When we turn to the New Testament, we meet evidence which is far more valuable but which is by no means straightforward. Jesus did not write a book. On the only occasion on which he is said in the New Testament to have written anything, he 'wrote on the ground with his finger' (John 8 : 6).

The New Testament was written in Greek. Its text has been examined with minute care, with the result that the Greek text which is used today in translations is more reliable than any known since the earliest days. The importance of this now seems obvious enough, yet in 1945 when a leading English writer, Ronald Knox, published a translation of the New Testament at the request of the Roman Catholic bishops of England and Wales it was based on the Latin translation, the Vulgate, completed by Jerome 1,540 years before (although Knox consulted the Greek).

Unless there is some absolutely stupendous discovery we shall never recover in complete detail the original text of the New Testament – the handwriting of Paul, Mark, Matthew, and so forth, or their secretaries,

on both sides of scrolls made of papyrus. Instead we
have to rely on copies made on vellum (probably
antelope skins) in the fourth century, specially on the
two magnificent copies known as the *Codex Vaticanus*
(in Rome) and the *Codex Siniaticus* (discovered in 1859
and now in the British Museum, London) – backed up,
or in some details corrected, by smaller sections written
on paper-like papyrus and dating from the third century
(all of them discovered within the last hundred years).

Using these ancient copies, scholars have agreed
on some major questions. Everything in Mark's gospel
after 16:8 is, as Today's English Version puts it, an
'old ending to the gospel' rather than the original
ending. (Did Mark stop at 16:8? Was his original ending lost before any other copy of his gospel had been
made? We do not know.) The story of the woman
caught in adultery in John's gospel (8:1-11) was added
to that gospel in some early copies. Various other verses
of the gospels are also absent from the earliest surviving manuscripts: they are printed in Today's English
Version in square brackets.

However, most of the questions answered by modern
study of the text have been comparatively minor. We
readily understand how easily small mistakes were
made when copying out the gospels by hand. We can
understand, too, how those who copied out the gospels
sometimes tried to make small improvements to the
wording in order to bring the gospels into line with
each other. But it is more surprising to realize how
long it took for scholars to agree about which were the
mistakes and the attempted improvements. The first
printing of the Greek New Testament was in 1516; the
text had been edited in a hurry by the famous scholar,
Erasmus. Four years later an edition prepared by

Spanish scholars under the direction of Cardinal Ximenes received the Pope's approval for publication. These texts were unsatisfactory, and even the revised edition edited by Robert Estienne with careful footnotes and printed in Paris in 1550 was still far from perfect – although that became known as the 'received text' and its reign was not broken until a German scholar, J. J. Griesbach, issued his edition in 1774-5. The most important contribution to the recovery of the Greek text which we use today was made by two English scholars, Westcott and Hort, who published the results of their work in 1881. Today's English Version is based on the Greek New Testament published in 1966 by the American Bible Society and its counterparts in Great Britain, Germany, and the Netherlands.

The text having been recovered as completely as possible, it is necessary to ask what the words mean. There will always be room for argument about many points, as can be seen by comparing any two of the translations of the Greek into English since William Tyndale's heroically pioneering effort, printed in 1526. But solid results have been achieved by modern study.

It often used to be assumed that the language used in the New Testament was a sacred and unique kind of Greek, 'the language of the Holy Spirit'. In fact it was the ordinary Greek of the day and most of it was not literary language but the common-or-garden, street-or-market, Greek of everyday informal speech or writing (*koine* Greek). The Greek of the last book in the Bible can justly be called barbarous, and the Greek of Mark's gospel is not all that much better. The meaning of the many phrases has been illuminated by the discovery of fragments of everyday letters in first-century rubbish dumps which are wonderfully preserved in the dryness of the sand in Egypt. But many scholars have gone further. They have researched as deeply as possible into the life of the Jews of Palestine in the first century. Far more is known about that Jewish background today than a hundred years ago. Attempts have been made to translate the sayings of Jesus back from Greek into the original language used, Aramaic. Detailed comparisons have been made between the sayings and the teachings of the Jewish rabbis and the Qumran monks. Experts do not always agree, but much light has been thrown on many problems in this way.

Such work on the text and the language has been only the beginning of the scholars' quest for the truth. There has been an enormous discussion about the relationship of the gospels to each other and to the real history of Jesus. This discussion will presumably never end. None of the gospels includes any explanation of how the author has treated the material available to him. In printed Bibles the gospels carry the names of four authors, but the earlier manuscripts did not give these. In fact curiosity and uncertainty surrounded the identity of the authors, and (as we shall see) various later writers had to attempt to supply the necessary information.

Anyone reading the gospels with any care will notice that they differ. The most used part of the whole Christian tradition is the Lord's Prayer. Two versions are given, by Luke (11:2-4) and Matthew (6:9-13). Luke's is shorter. It omits 'Our' before, and 'in heaven' after, 'Father'. It omits 'may your will be done on earth as it is in heaven'. It has different wording for the sentence beginning 'Forgive us . . .' and it omits the clause 'but keep us safe from the Evil One'. (Both versions omit 'For yours is the Kingdom . . .', evidently added by the Church.) Another famous passage is the Beatitudes: 'Happy are . . .' Here, too, Luke's version (6:20-23) is shorter than Matthew's (5:3-12). Most scholars think it likely that Luke's is the earlier version in each case.

Had it been a question of only a few passages being slightly different, it might have been argued reasonably that Jesus said similar but different things on similar but different occasions, and that in every case he has been reported accurately in the gospels. But the differences are much larger than that. Today's English Version is very conveniently printed in head-lined sections, and a note at the top of each section shows the parallels between the gospels. If these parallels are examined, any reader can see for himself how many and how big are the differences. Almost all who have taken the trouble to compare the gospels in this way have found it impossible to conclude that *all* the passages are completely accurate records of what was said and done. It seems far more sensible to conclude that the material has been edited. We all know that every TV programme or newspaper is edited, and the editorial line, slant, or bias, quite often shows up when we compare different programmes or news-papers; but the editorial process in the gospels seems to have been more substantial than anything we expect in responsible modern news-reporting.

Pieces of material have been gathered to make patterns. The most important example is that Matthew has collected into the Sermon on the Mount (chapters 5, 6 and 7) material which is scattered in Luke's gospel. A much smaller example is that Mark has collected three sayings, about salt (9:49, 50). Sometimes the pattern may not show itself on a first, quick reading, but it is there. For example, Mark 8:1-26 has just the same pattern as Mark 6:30-7:37 – feeding the thousands, crossing the lake, a dispute with the Pharisees, a conversation about bread, and a healing. Sometimes the significance of the pattern is not clear to us. We cannot be sure why Mark, or a Christian community before him, made the double pattern just mentioned: the most commonly accepted explanation is that the first pattern refers to feeding, leading, and healing Jews and the second pattern to feeding, leading, and healing Gentiles. But sometimes the editor of the gospel has added his own revealing touches. A striking example comes in the prayer of Jesus for his disciples in John, where Jesus says that 'this is eternal life: for men to know you, the only true God, and to know Jesus Christ, whom you sent' (17:3). By far the most likely explanation of that aside is that it expresses John's conviction about Jesus Christ. There seem to be similar introductions of a Christian title into the reports of the teaching of Jesus elsewhere in the gospels, for example: 'Anyone who gives you a drink of water because you belong to Christ will certainly receive his reward' (Mark 9:41).

At the end of Matthew's gospel Jesus says: 'Go . . . to all peoples everywhere and make them my disciples; baptize them in the name of the Father, the Son, and the Holy Spirit' (28:19). It seems impossible to reconcile this with the evidence in Paul's letters and in the Acts of the Apostles that there was delay and controversy in the Church before it was seen clearly that non-Jewish people ought to be welcomed to baptism – which in the early days was 'in the name of' the Lord Jesus, *not* of 'the Father, the Son, and the Holy Spirit'. The most reasonable verdict is that the wording at this point in Matthew's gospel is by Matthew. Many other examples of editorial touches in the gospels could be given, although of course there is no need to think that all the material in the gospels originated with their editors rather than with Jesus – and there is room for a great deal of legitimate disagreement about exactly which words are editorial, and which record the authentic voice of Jesus.

How, then, were the gospels put together?

It is now generally agreed that the earliest gospel in the New Testament was Mark's. Some people in the early centuries of the Church already saw this, but Augustine of Hippo (354-430) threw the weight of his authority behind the belief that the first gospel was Matthew's. The power of this belief was such that it was still accepted in 1776 when the German scholar J. J. Griesbach (whose work on the Greek text we have already noticed) published 'A Synopsis of the Gospels of Matthew, Mark, and Luke'. The word 'Synopsis' means that these three gospels look at things in roughly the same way, and from Griesbach's use of the word it has become customary to refer to these three as the 'Synoptic' gospels. Griesbach suggested that Mark used Matthew and Luke in addition to his own information, and he arranged the three gospels in an attempt to demonstrate this. Much work by later scholars (beginning with C. H. Weisse in 1838) had to be done before agreement was reached that in fact Matthew and Luke independently used Mark plus other material. But another argument put forward by Griesbach – that the fourth gospel, John's, must be separated from the other three – has stood the test of time. Countless attempts have been made to combine all four gospels in a harmony. It cannot be done without twisting the evidence, as we shall see in chapter 3 of this book.

When Matthew and Luke used Mark, they often

shortened his stories – as can be seen by comparing (for example) Mark's reports of healing miracles in his chapter 5 with the parallel passages in the other two Synoptic gospels. But Matthew and Luke also added much. Some of this material is common to them, and scholars call it 'Q' (from the German *Quelle*, meaning 'Source'). This material is, however, not used by Matthew and Luke in the same order or in precisely the same wording. Matthew tends to group together passages which Luke scatters. In addition to the differences caused by the different editorial treatments in Matthew and Luke, it is possible that they had before them different versions of Q. Many attempts have been made to reconstruct Q, but we cannot be sure that any material which is now found only in Matthew or Luke did *not* come from Q. All we can say with confidence is that Q consisted mainly of sayings of Jesus with stories leading up to these pronouncements when necessary. Matthew and Luke had to get most of their narrative from Mark or elsewhere.

In addition to their use of Mark and Q, Matthew and Luke both presented their own material. This is referred to by scholars as M and L. We cannot be sure where it came from. Presumably some of it was based on research; Luke claims to have 'carefully studied all these matters from their beginning' (1:3). But it seems reasonable to suppose that some of this special material was the traditional teaching of the Christian communities to which Matthew and Luke belonged, and some was added because they thought it appropriate. It is not possible to tell what notes they used. Efforts have been made to reconstruct the stages by which M and L were compiled, but all such efforts are guesswork. However, we do know that Matthew and Luke felt free to arrange their material in different orders, from which it would appear that Mark's order was not felt to be completely accurate and Q's order was not felt to matter very much. Indeed there have been suggestions that Matthew, and perhaps Mark before him, arranged his material so as to provide lessons for the year in the Church's worship – but here again we are in the realm of guess-work.

The sayings of Jesus about divorce in the gospels are not only relevant to human problems but are also illuminating about how the gospels were written. In Matthew's gospel there are two references to divorce (5:31-32; 19:1-12). Apparently Matthew has included them both because he has taken the first from Q (see Luke 16:18), while the second is an enlarged version of Mark 10:1-12. The failure to combine these passages seems strange, but Matthew has taken care to add one clause which is neither in Mark nor in Luke. This is the clause here printed in italics. 'Any man who divorces his wife, *and she has not been unfaithful*, commits adultery if he marries some other woman' (19:9). It looks as if Matthew, or the special material on which he relied, added this phrase because the absolute prohibition of remarriage after divorce – 'man must not separate . . . what God has joined together' (Mark 10:9) – had already proved too austere an ideal to be a practical law.

Mark also seems to have added a claim to the original prohibition: 'in the same way, the woman who divorces her husband and marries another man commits adultery' (10:12). This can be regarded as an addition to the original saying of Jesus because it was absolutely impossible for a Jewish woman in Palestine to divorce her husband under any circumstances. Mark seems to have adjusted the prohibition to

the legal situation in the place where he was writing
(probably Rome) and where women had rather more
freedom.

The conclusion that both Mark and Matthew changed
the form of the saying of Jesus about divorce in
order to fit the circumstances of their own readers is
an example of the detective work which modern
scholars have applied to the gospels. Their most
ambitious method is 'form criticism'. This is a method
of probing the gospels which was developed by the
German scholars, Martin Dibelius and Rudolf Bultmann, in the 1920s. First it probes the form of the
passage in front of us in the gospels. The fact that
Today's English Version is printed in sections each
with its own headline helps us to see that each of the
gospels is made up of sections like pearls on a string,
and that each section has its own shape. A story may
lead up to a miracle or to a pronouncement, and any
details left in it build up to that. The story has acquired
this 'form' by being told. So the hope of the 'form
critics' is that by studying the form of the story they
may be able to detect how the story has changed over
the years since the original events of the life of Jesus.
This method of studying the gospels has had some
spectacularly successful results, although its prac-
titioners have tended to be over-confident.

'Form criticism' has been one of the methods used in
the attempt to discover which of the teachings attributed to Jesus in the gospels really came from him.
Many critical scholars work with the method known
as the 'criterion of dissimilarity'. This means that a
saying attributed to Jesus should be regarded as the
creation of the Christians unless it can be made to
seem highly probable that the Christians could *not* have

made it up. And certainly the case for the authenticity of a saying can be greatly strengthened in that way. The trouble is that it is illogical to suppose that Jesus never said things which the Christians could also have said. For example, 'Do not worry about tomorrow, it will have enough worries of its own' (Matthew 6:34) is a piece of wisdom which could have been spoken by many millions – including Jesus.

The story of the trial and crucifixion (the 'Passion') of Jesus occupies a place by itself. Anyone reading Mark's gospel will be struck by the amount of detail given in chapters 14 and 15, covering a few hours, compared with the rest of the material. Anyone comparing these chapters with Matthew's chapters 26 and 27 and with Luke's chapters 22 and 23 will see how much all three gospels have in common here, again compared with the remainder. There is even an overlap between these gospels and John's. The explanation seems to be that the narrative of the Passion of Jesus was preserved by the Church with a special care.

Looking at the story of the Passion helps us to see what the rest of the material is not. *It is not a biography*. Little attention is paid to the order in which most of the events or sayings should be placed; most of the links between section and section are left vague. In other words, we do not possess a chronological framework for the life of Jesus – although we are given a very simple outline putting a few events in order. If we were reading a modern biography such a disregard of time would be maddening, because we should expect a modern biography to tell us about the development of its subject's character, step by step. However, the gospels do not set out to inform us about the psychology of Jesus. It is only John's gospel that gives us many passages where Jesus is talking about himself, and that gospel is furthest from being biographical in the modern sense. The other gospels show us Jesus in action – and mostly they leave us guessing why he acted. But even the accounts of the activity of Jesus are strictly limited. We are told very little except about a single year – for that is the length of the public work of Jesus according to the Synoptic gospels, although John's gospel makes it two and a half years. The personal background of Jesus is left in some obscurity. Because we have no other evidence, we shall always know far less about Jesus the man than we should like to know.

The dates when the gospels were written have been much debated. Some scholars have suggested dates far removed from the historical Jesus. But in 1935 the existence of a fragment of papyrus containing some verses of chapter 18 of John in the John Rylands Library, Manchester, was made known. It had come from Egypt. Various tests have convinced the experts that this copy of John's gospel was made early in the second century. This discovery suggests that the gospel was written by the end of the first century, although the gospel itself suggests that it was not written much before this since is embodies a richly developed type of Christianity. It is commonly held that Mark's gospel was written about 65. The gospels of Matthew and Luke are usually dated between 70 and 90, but the collection of material called Q is presumably about as old as Mark's gospel, if not older. If these dates are roughly right they leave a gap of thirty-five years between the death of Jesus and the earliest of the gospels. Some evidence about Jesus is supplied by Paul's surviving correspondence. The earliest of this, the First Letter to the Thessalonians, almost certainly comes from the winter of 50-51, so that the gap is narrowed to some twenty years. Such dates bring us closer to the events being described than some sceptics have suggested, but we are not as close as we should like.

The greatest obstacle in recovering a reliable portrait of the historical Jesus is, however, the fact that these gospels were all written by ardent believers. So they assure us, and so they are – from beginning to end. This means that we have no *neutral* evidence. A question then arises about the extent to which the gospels are *objective*, telling us what really took place.

We cannot help being worried by the frequent remoteness of the gospels from modern forms of historical writing. For example, the very first chapter of Mark's gospel brings us slap up against six features of the first-century world of thought: (1) events took place as prophesied in the Old Testament, and the work of John the Baptist had been foretold by a Jewish prophet centuries before; (2) God's voice could speak; (3) God's spirit could come down like a dove, directly from heaven; (4) Satan tested people; (5) evil spirits or demons possessed them, causing diseases; (6) these demons could speak.

It is not surprising that many scholars have used the word 'mythological' to describe the strange world of the gospels, and it is natural that many thoughtful people who have wanted to make clear the relevance to modern man have emphasized the necessity of 'demy-thologizing'. This challenge has been voiced with a special force by the German scholar, Rudolf Bultmann. The demythologizing programme proposed by Bultmann has caused a great controversy which is not over yet, but probably about all Christians would agree that there *is* a problem here – because those who compiled the gospels simply did not write in the way a modern author would today. The gospels cannot be understood without some interpretation, linking the world of Old Testament prophecy with the news on television, the voice of God from heaven with the modern interest in psychology, the symbolism of the first century with our images, the first-century understanding of evil with our understanding, the first-century belief in demon possession with modern medicine. Probably many individual events which were depicted by the gospels in that first-century style and framework cannot now be completely reconstructed to fit our conventions, for often we simply do not know, and cannot know, 'what really happened' – when by 'really' we mean 'as we can be sure'. For example, we do not know exactly what happened when Jesus was baptized. But our duty is inescapable. Because we are modern people, we must ask what is most likely to have been the general shape of events which really happened. And because we are modern people, we must ask what the general shape of those events means to us today. The truth is that we have no alternative. In no other way can we treat those events as real – and in no other way can we begin to understand them. We are modern, and we cannot jump out of our skins back to the first century.

Obviously, many difficult problems are involved. For example, just because an Old Testament prophet hoped for an event, it is *not* impossible that the event took place in the first century. And just because the Old Testament was quoted in the first century to show the meaning of an event, it is *not* certain that the meaning for us must be completely opposite. But sometimes our modern task is comparatively simple – as when we read in Matthew's gospel (21:5) a quotation from the prophet Zechariah (9:9):

> 'Tell the city of Zion,
>   Now your king is coming to you.
> He is gentle and rides on a donkey,
>   on a colt, the foal of a donkey.'

Matthew believed that this prophecy must have been fulfilled exactly when Jesus rode triumphantly into Jerusalem. He reads Zechariah as referring to a donkey *and* a colt; so he tells us that 'they brought the donkey and the colt, threw their cloaks over them, and Jesus got on.' But it requires no great effort in modern detective work to see that Matthew has misunderstood the quotation. Zechariah was referring to only one animal, a young donkey or colt, symbolizing a peaceful journey and chosen instead of a war-horse. He was not expecting the King to ride two donkeys as Matthew says. We can therefore regard Mark's account as more probable, not only because it is earlier but also because it produces only one animal, a colt (11:1-11) – which does *not* mean that Jesus had forgotten all about Zechariah's prophecy when he chose to make his great entrance in this way.

These, then, are the main conclusions of modern scholarship about the methods open to us as we examine the evidence about Jesus. Up to a point, these results are positive and helpful. We have discovered much about the gospels, their origins, and their value. But many people find the results disappointing. The scholarly discussion has many of the characteristics of the games people play in scholarly circles. It usually concerns details rather than embarrassingly important topics; it is often influenced by fashions rather than facts; and it is often accompanied by a considerable display of confidence that one scholar's guesses are facts. All this is to be expected and would not matter – were it not that the subject of the debate is Jesus, a subject still felt to be important by millions who are impatient with the scholars' games.

Many people are now aware of the seriousness of the problems arising in the modern critical study of the New Testament. They know that Jesus has been described as an impatient and arrogant young man, as a political rebel, as a fanatic with illusions about the end of the world, as a myth belonging to the ancient 'mystery' religions, as a teacher no bigger than the religion around him in Palestine, and so forth. They probably do not find any of these theories very convincing, but they ask what the critical scholars have to put in the place of such theories. They find much information about what the early Christians believed. They find many warnings about the difficulty of getting at the facts behind the Christian beliefs. But they do not find what they are really looking for. There seems to be a Jesus-sized gap at the end of these critical studies, and many people complain about the scholars as Mary Magdalene complains in John's gospel (20:13): 'They have taken my Lord away, and I do not know where they have put him!'

The result is that many people who admire or follow Jesus decide to ignore the critical approach to the New Testament. They read the gospels for the inspiration they can give morally and spiritually, without bothering about awkward questions of fact. This is all very well, but the obvious danger is that their picture of Jesus will be unreal and sentimental – and we return to the point made at the beginning of this chapter: such pictures will not survive for long in the modern atmosphere of frank criticism. In the long run Christianity has no future if Jesus and the truth are thought to be on opposite sides.

The religious situation of today plainly demands that the honest, critical study of the gospels should be carried forward to the point where the truth it reaches is as big as the subject under discussion. The many valuable insights and constructive suggestions of the critical scholars need to be developed into a truthful and therefore convincing modern account of the real Jesus. A great deal of such work has already been done, and has aroused the gratitude of those familiar with it – but it needs to be made far more widely known.

If justice is to be done by modern man to the Jesus phenomenon, the recognition of the literary and historical realities has to be combined with the acknowledgement of the titanic impact of this unique man and the spiritual splendour of the movement which he started. And then a decision must be made about the meaning and truth of the message of Jesus. It is not reasonable to expect scholars whose skill lies in the investigation of literary and historical problems to make that decision for us. It is a moral and spiritual decision; and it is life-transforming. All that we can reasonably ask is that the facts given us should fit the size of our questions. That request is reasonable because the men who wrote the New Testament certainly thought that the facts which they knew were enough to arouse faith, for life and for death.

They wrote what they had learned about Jesus – what he said, what he did, what he was. They wrote with burning hearts and keen minds. They were different men, they saw differently, and their testimonies were different, but they had all felt the force of one man

B

– who to them all was more than any other man. We live in a world very different from theirs, and each one of us approaches this matter differently. But the men who wrote the New Testament still challenge us to make our responses to the Lord they had met. For to them, he was in his own person the best answer to the question which Pilate asked in the high drama of the trial of Jesus in John's gospel (18:38): 'And what is truth?'

2

THE CHRISTIANS' LORD

These 27 books now printed in it were not the only candidates for inclusion in the New Testament. They were selected by the Christian Church, and it is not usually recognized how long it took for the Church to agree on the 'canon' or official contents of the New Testament. For the decisive verdict was that of the great teacher of orthodoxy, Athanasius of Alexandria, in a letter in 367. Within thirty years a council of church leaders at Hippo in North Africa taught the same 'canon'; and so did the famous Bishop of Hippo, Augustine.

The first list of the contents of the New Testament as received by the church in Rome that has come down to us was probably completed between 180 and 200. Because it was discovered in 1740 by a scholar named Muratori, it is called the Muratorian Canon. One of its purposes seems to have been to answer the challenge put by Marcion, a wealthy shipowner and lay theologian, in Rome shortly before 150. Marcion proposed a New Testament consisting of Luke's gospel and ten of Paul's letters, all edited to conform to his own teachings. Another challenge came, as we shall shortly see, from the gospels written by minority groups of Christians during the second century.

The debate on the contents of the New Testament heard many more respectable voices raised in controversy – not only about comparatively minor items such as the letters to Timothy and Titus or the letters of Peter, James, John, and Jude, but also about three major books: the Gospel of John, the Letter to the

Hebrews, and the Revelation to John. Books which could be treated as inspired writings included the long First Letter of Clement (a call from Rome to Corinth, urging obedience to the congregation's properly appointed leaders, almost certainly written within the first century), the Letter of Barnabas, the *Shepherd* of Hermas, the Acts of Paul, the Preaching of Peter, and the Revelation to Peter. The fourth-century *Codex Siniaticus* included the Letter of Barnabas and part of the *Shepherd*.

All this indicates that it took centuries before the Christian Church had finally made up its mind about what the New Testament was. On the other hand, the general acceptance of the Gospels of Mark, Matthew, and Luke and of the ten main letters of Paul took place in the second century: and the process began within the period covered by the New Testament. In our gospels when 'the Scriptures' are mentioned, the Old Testament is meant (Mark 12:24; Luke 24:27, etc.) – but some Christian writings were soon put on the same level, as is indicated in what is almost certainly the New Testament's latest book, the Second Letter from Peter. The author refers (3:15-16) to 'our dear brother Paul' who 'wrote to you, using the wisdom God gave him . . . There are some difficult things in his letters which ignorant and unstable people explain falsely, *as they do with other passages of the Scriptures.* So they bring on their own destruction.'

Why were these books chosen as the Scriptures of the New Testament? There seem to have been two main reasons. No doubt there were other reasons, such as the prestige of an apostle's name. But in the ancient world it was a well-known practice for authors to use the names of great men of the past rather than their own, and this seems to have been regarded generally as an example of humility rather than of deceit. Many books bearing the apostles' names were in the end excluded from the New Testament.

It seems clear that the first reason for choosing them was that these books had the power to express the strength of Christian feeling in worship and life, where Jesus was adored as the eternal Lord.

The Christian worship reflected in the New Testament possessed a great vitality. Paul reminds the Corinthian Christians in his first letter (14:26): 'When you meet for worship, one man has a hymn, another a teaching, another a revelation from God, another a message in strange tongues, and still another the explanation of what is said.' The man who wrote the Letter to the Hebrews could not understand how anyone who had taken part in such worship could ever cease to be a Christian. 'They were once in God's light. They tasted heaven's gift and received their share of the Holy Spirit. They knew from experience that God's word is good, and they had felt the powers of the coming age. And then they fell away!' (6:4-6) He recalls his readers to their experience of the union of heaven and earth in Christian worship. 'You have come to Mount Zion and to the city of the living God, the heavenly Jerusalem, with its thousands of angels. You have come to the joyful gathering of God's oldest sons, whose names are written in heaven. You have come to God, who is the judge of all men, and to the spirits of righteous men made perfect. You have come to Jesus . . .' (12:22-24).

The fervently personal praise of the unseen Lord Jesus was what was distinctive about Christian worship in its early years. The recently discovered scrolls of the Essene monks at Qumran provide an illuminating contrast. The man who founded that community was certainly honoured in it as 'the Teacher of Righteousness' – yet in all the surviving scrolls he is never once named. The followers of Jesus were nicknamed 'Christians' because they were always talking about Jesus as *Christos* or 'Messiah': he was the deliverer promised to Israel. The Acts of the Apostles records that 'it was at Antioch that the disciples were first called Christians' (11:26). The title was kept when many pagans to whom Jewish hopes meant little became Christians. Some use was also still made of the mysterious Jewish title 'Son of Man', to be discussed later (see page 172). But the title which now meant more was *Kurios* or 'Lord'. The God of Israel was *Kurios* in the Greek version of the Old Testament. The divine revealers and saviours of the pagan mystery religions were 'lords'. And the Roman Emperor was often called 'Lord God'.

In the reign of Domitian (81-96) the use of this title became compulsory, and those who refused to use it in honouring the Emperor became liable to execution. It was probably under this tyrant that John put at the end of his gospel the faith of Thomas in Jesus: 'My Lord and my God!' (20:28) – and the Revelation to John proclaimed Jesus as 'King of kings and Lord of lords' (19:16). That faith was expressed in the acts of worship performed by the Christians – as is shown in the famous letter from a Roman governor in Asia Minor, Pliny the Younger, to the Emperor Trajan about 112.

Pliny asked the Emperor what he ought to do about the Christians. A tiresome number had been brought before him, although all had either denied that they had any connection with Christianity or had proved that they had given it up by offering a token sacrifice (incense and wine) before the images of the Emperor and the gods and by cursing Christ. Those who admitted that they had once been Christians did, however, tell the Roman officials that the popular idea that Christian worship consisted of atheism, incest, and cannibalism was incorrect, and when two Christian deaconesses were examined under torture they, too, revealed nothing more than what Pliny called 'squalid superstition'. Pliny now passed on to the Emperor the account he had gathered of Christian worship. Christians attended a meeting before dawn on a particular day (no doubt Sunday was meant), sang a hymn 'to Christ as a god', and took an oath to abstain from crime. They then dispersed, but it had been their custom to meet again for an ordinary meal until there had been an imperial edict forbidding secret societies.

In his reply the Emperor told Pliny not to organize a campaign against Christians but to punish those who were properly accused and found guilty and who remained obstinate. In fact Christianity remained an offence carrying the death penalty. Quite apart from the popular belief that Christians were atheists and cannibals, the Roman Empire did not want in its boundaries anyone who treated an executed criminal as a divine lord.

We have in the New Testament several examples of these hymns to Christ. In the Revelation to John, some of the songs which John hears in his vision of heaven sound like snatches of hymns familiar to him and his first readers from their worship on earth:

'You were killed, and by your death
    you bought men for God,
      from every tribe, language, nation, and race.
  You have made them a kingdom of priests
        to serve our God,
      and they shall rule on earth' (5 : 9-10).

'The Lamb who was killed is worthy
    to receive power, wealth, wisdom, and strength,
    honour, glory, and praise! . . .
To him who sits on the throne, and to the Lamb,
    be praise and honour, glory and might,
    forever and ever!' (5:12-13)

In the First Letter to Timothy there is a definite
quotation from a hymn about Christ's glory:

'He appeared in human form,
        was shown to be right by the Spirit,
            and was seen by angels.
    He was preached among the nations,
        was believed in the world,
            and was taken up to heaven' (3:16).

The same theme was worked out more fully by an
unknown poet whose magnificent hymn was quoted
by Paul to the Christians in Philippi.

'He always had the very nature of God,
    but he did not think that by force he should try to
    become equal with God.
Instead, of his own free will he gave it all up,
    and took the nature of a servant.
He became like man,
    and appeared in human likeness.
He was humble and walked the path of obedience
    to death
    – his death on the cross.
For this reason God raised him to the highest
    place above,
    and gave him the name that is greater
    than any other name.
And so, in honour of the name of Jesus,
    all beings in heaven, on earth, and in the world
    below will fall on their knees,
    and all will openly proclaim that Jesus Christ is the
    Lord,
    to the glory of God the Father' (2:6-11).

Some scholars believe that at least two other passages
in the New Testament include quotations from similar
hymns, although in Today's English Version they are

not printed as poetry. These possible hymns are to be found in the Letter to the Colossians (1:15-20), and in the Gospel of John (1:1-14).

Whether or not the famous prologue to John's gospel (with its claim that Jesus was 'the same as God') is based on a hymn, we can be certain from the evidence in Paul's letters that a highly exalted estimate of Jesus was widespread in the Church before the gospels. Before Mark, Matthew, Luke, or John wrote, Christians had reached the astounding conclusion that Jesus, who had lived like a servant and died like a criminal, had always had the very nature of God. This is the faith expressed with great power throughout the fourth gospel. But it seems highly probable that Mark had at least some of these ideas in his mind when he began to write 'the Good News about Jesus Christ, the Son of God' – and when he had the army officer say after the death of Jesus: 'This man was really the Son of God!' (15:39) Matthew believed that Jesus had been given 'all authority in heaven and on earth' (28:18). When Luke in his second volume, the Acts of the Apostles, made Peter say that Jesus had been 'raised to the right side of God' (2:33), he was surely voicing his own faith too. And we can be sure that the four gospels would not have been accepted in the Church if their authors had seemed to be reaching a conclusion about Jesus Christ less than the conclusions which Christians were already singing in their worship about 'the name that is greater than any other name'.

All four gospels, then, were written by and for people who adored Jesus as the eternal Lord. They were written from faith to faith.

But we must face the fact that the worship of Jesus as the divine Lord who had taken the nature of a servant could easily be connected with a myth which was very popular among the Gentiles to whom Paul and other Christians preached in the first century. This was the myth of the Lord, Revealer, or Redeemer who had given men knowledge (in Greek, *gnosis* – always a key term). He had dwelt in the upper sphere of light but out of pure compassion had descended to earth, into the sphere of darkness, in order to communicate the secrets and the powers of the eternal light and life. After accomplishing this mission triumphantly, he had returned to his heavenly home. This theme ran through many of the Near Eastern 'mystery' religions of the time, and it was a theme that was developed into a very powerful heresy by the Christian 'Gnostics' who had already begun in the first century and who flourished in the second century.

In the long and bitter conflict with Gnosticism, the Church defined the dangers of the myth which was so attractive. The myth made no contact with real history: the divine Lord of the Gnostics only seemed to be human. It made no demand for a real decision: there was no objection to calling the mythological Lord now by one name, now by another. And it made no contribution to the everyday moral struggle: the myth had no moral consequences. Once we become aware of the popularity and danger of this myth, we have to ask whether the Christians of the first century, singing their hymns and welcoming their gospels, were merely changing the historical Jesus into a Gnostic myth.

To find the answer, we have to turn to the second main reason why these four gospels and the other twenty-three books were received into the New Testament. *They fought any tendency to heresy by recalling the historical Jesus with his exclusive claims*

*and his ethical demands; they checked mythology
by morality.*

We can watch this fight in (for example) the first
letter of John. These letters almost certainly come
from the same pen as John's gospel, and of all the
books in the New Testament the Gospel of John is
closest to the Gnostic myth; 'God is light' sounds like
Gnosticism. Yet the whole letter is a blast of the
trumpet against the beginnings of Gnosticism. To
have the Spirit of God it is necessary to say that 'Jesus
Christ came as a human being' (4:2); it is necessary to
hold that 'Jesus Christ is the one who came' (5:6); and
in a very practical fashion it is necessary to live and love
'just as Jesus Christ did' (2:6).

The Letter to the Ephesians shows that even the
hymns of the Christians had a practical message.
The letter quotes:

> 'Wake up, sleeper,
>   and rise from the dead!
> And Christ will shine upon you' (5:14).

Then it immediately adds: 'So pay close attention to
how you live' – and it goes on to discuss temperance
and mutual respect, with the duties of wives, husbands,
children, parents, slaves, and masters. And in the
Second Letter to Timothy comes the last of the early
Christian hymns that we shall quote. It is a hymn about
following the one Lord to a martyr's death – not
about the emotional excitement of a myth.

> 'If we have died with him,
>   we shall also live with him.
> If we continue to endure,
>   we shall also rule with him.
> If we deny him,
>   he also will deny us:
> If we are not faithful,
>   he remains faithful,
>   because he cannot be false to himself (2:11-13).

Paul preached a Lord who was historical, exclusive, and ethical. As he wrote in his first letter to the Christians in Corinth, 'we proclaim Christ on the cross' (1:23). 'When I came to you, my brothers, to preach God's secret truth to you, I did not use long words and great learning. For I made up my mind to forget everything while I was with you except Jesus Christ, and especially his death on the cross' (2:1, 2). He made it equally clear that the victory of Christ was known not through mythology but through events: 'I want to remind you, brothers, of the Good News which I preached to you . . .' (15:1-8). This letter explicitly contrasts Paul's message with any knowledge of mythical lords. 'Even if there are so-called "gods," whether in heaven or on earth, and even though there are many of these "gods" and "lords," yet there is for us only one God, the Father, who is the creator of all things, and for whom we live; and there is only one Lord, Jesus Christ, through whom all things were created, and through whom we live' (8:5, 6). And the Christians in Corinth are told firmly that no 'knowledge' is to excuse any lack of sensitivity to 'your brother for whom Christ died' (8:10, 11).

When we are dazzled by the skill with which Paul used the language of the pagan 'mystery' religions familiar to Gentiles such as the Corinthians, we need to remember that his own background was that of a strictly educated Jewish Pharisee. Every student of Jewish religion was trained to hold his teacher in great reverence and to remember what he taught without writing it down. In his turn every rabbi was expected to quote *his* teachers in order to justify his opinions. Plainly Paul had an attitude to the historical Jesus very different from a normal student's relation to his rabbis – and Jesus himself broke through the con-

ventions of the rabbinic tradition. But it is also plain
that much of the rabbinic discipline stayed with Paul.

It has been argued by those who have stressed the
mythological nature of Paul's beliefs that his interest in
the historical Jesus was confined to the two events of the
cross and the resurrection – just enough to set the myth
in motion. And certainly those two facts dominated
Paul's thought. It is also the case that Paul's surviving
letters seldom quote Jesus and seldom mention biographical facts. On the other hand, it is possible to
reach a fairly full understanding of the character of
Jesus in action by reading Paul's letters. And Paul's
first letter to Corinth – which in its account of Christian
love in chapter 13 gives a little portrait of Jesus
– shows that he did not feel at liberty to invoke the
authority of 'the Lord' for anything he wished to
teach, without regard to history. 'For married people I
have a command, not my own but the Lord's . . . To
the others I say (I, myself, not the Lord) . . . Now, the
matter about the unmarried: I do not have a command
from the Lord, but I give my opinion as one who by the
Lord's mercy is worthy of trust' (7:10, 12, 25). 'The
Lord has ordered that those who preach the gospel
should get their living from it' (9:14).

What does Paul mean when he says 'the Lord'? He
means a Jesus who is alive and no mere figure of
history. This Lord is able to speak to Paul, although so
far as we know the two men never met in the
ordinary sense. He writes: 'From the Lord I received
the teaching that I passed on to you: that the Lord
Jesus, on the night he was betrayed, took the bread . . .'
(11:23). It follows that Paul's relationship with the
Lord is something stranger than the relationship with
a dead hero which can exist in the memory of a
living man. Jesus is the living Lord. But it does not

follow that in Paul's thought the living Lord could make pronouncements having no link with history.

In the earliest Christian document that has survived, Paul's First Letter to the Thessalonians, we read: 'Do not restrain the Holy Spirit; do not despise inspired messages' (5:19, 20). But this document puts the emphasis on the instruction which follows immediately: 'put all things to the test.' And it makes completely clear Paul's insistence that one of the tests of the value of an inspired message is whether or not it conforms to the Good News which God entrusted to him in the course of history (2:4). That history is why he now claims 'the authority of the Lord Jesus' (4:2, 5:27).

The history to which Paul appealed included experience which he interpreted as a direct encounter with the living Lord Jesus, so that writing to the Galatians a few years later he could boast: 'When [God] decided to reveal his Son to me, so that I might preach the Good News about him to the Gentiles, I did not go to anyone for advice' (1:15, 16). But that should not be taken as implying that the Good News preached by Paul relied entirely on his own mysticism or contained no historical information. He insisted to the contrary when writing to the Corinthians. And in the first letter to the Thessalonians (4:15), Paul was glad to be able to appeal to a saying of Jesus. ('This is the Lord's teaching that we tell you: we who are alive on the day the Lord comes will not go ahead of those who have died.')

Again and again in Paul's teaching, a passage which seems to be plunging deep into mythology regains its footing in the history of Jesus and his disciples. An example comes in this letter to the Galatians (4:3-6). 'We . . . were slaves of the ruling spirits of the universe, before we reached spiritual maturity. But when the right time finally came, God sent his own Son. He came as the son of a human mother, and lived under the Jewish Law . . . so that we might become God's sons. To show that you are his sons, God sent the Spirit of his Son into our hearts, the Spirit who cries, "Father, my Father".' The word which Paul uses for 'Father' is *Abba*, the word used by the historical Jesus.

The Revelation to John takes a freer attitude to the words of the Lord than Paul allowed himself. After an ecstatic vision, a Christian prophet writes: 'On the Lord's day the Spirit took control of me, and I heard a loud voice, that sounded like a trumpet, speaking behind me' (1:10). He gives messages from the Lord which are trumpet-calls to the churches in seven places of which (we may guess) the historical Jesus never heard. We know from the *Didache* (a document which comes probably from Syria at the end of the first, or the beginning of the second, century) that there were many Christian prophets touring the congregations with messages from the Lord. But even this ecstatic prophecy is still rooted in history and in morality. What mattered supremely to the Christians was that they could know Jesus as their contemporary, their living Lord. 'Don't be afraid! I am the first and the last. I am the living one! I was dead, but look, I am alive forever and ever. I have authority over death and the world of the dead.' So it is said in the Revelation to John (1:17, 18). But such a thing could not have been said without the belief that there had been an event in history, when 'Jesus Christ, the faithful witness, the firstborn Son . . . was raised from death' (1:5).

It is clear that the messages thought to flow from the living Lord were not expected to contradict the kind of thing the historical Jesus had said. Thus the author of the *Didache* shrewdly advised his readers not to believe 'prophets' if they ordered meals in the name of the Lord! We can be confident that the Revelation to John would have been even more suspect than it in fact was (there was prolonged uncertainty before it was finally received into the New Testament), had it ended with an appeal for money.

For many years the words of innumerable preachers and a few letter-writers seemed enough to spread this message, quoting the deeds and words of Jesus. In the Acts of the Apostles we are given an example of a sermon which ends with a saying of Jesus not found in any of the surviving gospels. Paul tells the elders of Ephesus to remember the words that the Lord Jesus himself said, 'There is more happiness in giving than in receiving' (20:35). Collections of the sayings of Jesus would be made to assist this work. They were notes for preachers. There would be a particular need of an account of the trial and death of Jesus. Paul's First Letter to the Corinthians shows that at the centre of Christian worship was an act when the Lord's death was proclaimed (11:26). So the remembrance of that death and of the events leading up to it would be very frequent, and gradually fixed in one narrative. Another reason why the Passion of Jesus had to be recorded was, no doubt, the need to answer the constant questions of inquirers and opponents: why had the Christians' Lord met a criminal's death? Thus the materials now composing our gospels grew like a coral strand in the ocean. But the gospels themselves were not yet needed.

It is clear that there were also collections of quotations from 'the Scriptures' (meaning the Old

Testament) which were believed to foretell the life, death, and victory of Jesus. Many such quotations are to be found in Paul's letters, in the gospels, and in the Acts of the Apostles, and there is enough of a pattern in their use to indicate that they had been collected and arranged for the convenience of Christians. The quotations come from the Greek version, the Septuagint, and not from the original Hebrew. This is sometimes important; for example, Matthew 1:23 quotes Isaiah 7:14 as 'the virgin will become pregnant and give birth to a son' in accordance with the Greek version (or one meaning of it), although the Hebrew clearly referred to a 'young woman'. Sometimes the quotation is torn from its original context and given an artificial meaning: the Isaiah quotation just mentioned is a case in point. Sometimes small mistakes are made which might have been avoided had the Christians been accustomed always to look things up in the Old Testament. For example, the second sentence of Mark's gospel says impressively 'as the prophet Isaiah had written' – before giving a passage from Malachi and a slightly inaccurate Isaianic quotation. But on the whole the Christian collections of Old Testament testimonies did root the Christian faith in the faith of Israel, and embodied much hard and brave thought.

Writing to the Corinthians, Paul says that Christ died and was raised to life 'as written in the Scriptures' – which implies that his readers would be able to recognize the relevant prophecies in the Old Testament. But there was as yet no idea that Paul's letters would themselves become holy scriptures to the Christians, and would need supplementing by gospels. There are countless references to this stage of oral teaching in Paul's letters and in the Acts of the Apostles. There is also one in the Letter to the Hebrews (2:3, 4): 'The

Lord himself first announced this salvation, and those who heard him proved to us that it is true. At the same time God added his witness to theirs by doing signs of power, wonders, and many kinds of miracles. He also distributed the gifts of the Holy Spirit according to his will.'

From the closing years of the second century we have a reflection of the common trust in the disciplined memory behind the spoken word. Someone who had known the historical Jesus, or who had known one of the elders in touch with the first disciples, was likely to be more authoritative than any book. Papias, Bishop of Hierapolis in Asia Minor (Turkey), said as much in his *Exposition of the Lord's Sayings* – a book which has been lost, but which is quoted at the end of Book III in the *Ecclesiastical History* of Eusebius.

He wrote: 'I shall spare no trouble to present all that I once learned well from the presbyters and remembered well, together with my own explanations, since I can vouch for this truth. For, unlike most people, I took delight not in those who talk much but in those who teach the truth; not in those who relate strange teachings but in those who record the teachings which are given by the Lord to faith and derived from the truth itself. But if I met anyone who had been a follower of the elders, I was accustomed to ask about the sayings of the elders: what Andrew or Peter had said, or Philip or Thomas or James or John or Matthew or any other of the Lord's disciples, and what Aristion and John the Elder, disciples of the Lord, say. For I do not regard what comes from books as so valuable to me as what comes from a living and abiding voice.'

But there came a time when – to meet the needs of the Church for testimony to the eternal Lord who was also the historical Jesus with his austerely moral message – there had to be the gospels. Obviously it would have been best if the apostles had themselves written gospels. In his *First Apology*, which was the first systematic attempt to explain Christian practices and doctrines to non-Christians, Justin Martyr (a Christian teacher in Rome, writing in about 155) said that 'on the day called Sunday the memoirs of the apostles or the writings of the prophets' were read to the assembled Christians. But in another book, his *Dialogue with Trypho*, Justin had to refer to 'memoirs' written by 'the apostles and those who followed them'. For although many gospels claimed apostolic authority, it is almost certain that not one was in fact written by an apostle, and anyone reading them could tell that they were not the usual kind of memoirs. Accordingly many Christians felt free to supply the need.. Justin's own writings quote a number of other 'sayings of Jesus' as well as sayings found in one or other of the gospels of our New Testament. Luke's gospel begins: 'Many have done their best to write a report of the things that have taken place among us. They wrote what we have been told by those who saw these things from the beginning and proclaimed the message.'

Of the gospels to which Luke refers, only Mark's has survived. Justin quotes it as 'the memoirs of Peter'. But there were also many other gospels written after Luke's. For example, quotations have survived in Clement of Alexandria, Origen, and Jerome from the Gospel of the Hebrews, including this fine example of Christian mysticism: 'He that seeks will not rest until he finds; and he that has found shall marvel; and he that has marvelled shall reign; and he that has reigned shall rest.' But the gospel clearly comes from the second century and from the austere group of Jewish Christians called the Ebionites (see page 177).

Most of the surviving gospels not in the New Testament come from the Gnostics, whom we have already encountered (see page 42). Their Jesus says many of the same things, and does many of the same things, that could be read in popular pagan religious writing of the second and third Christian centuries. For example, he speaks with contempt about the body, and specially about unredeemed women. A good many of these Gnostic gospels have survived in whole or in part. Among them, the Gospel of Thomas, the Gospel of Philip, and the Gospel of Truth were found in an Egyptian village in 1945-6, and a part of the Gospel of Peter was found in another in 1886-7. Such gospels are justly called 'apocryphal', for they are of little historical value. Some of the material in them is also in the New Testament gospels (and is probably always derived from them), and conceivably some of their own material may preserve authentic sayings of Jesus. But some material of this type (for example, about the miracles which Jesus performed while playing as a child in Nazareth) is full of tall stories which are evidently legends – and many of the 'sayings of Jesus' given in the Gospels of Thomas, Philip, Peter, and so forth, clearly reflect Gnostic views.

One of the reasons why there was such prolonged uncertainty about what should be included in the New Testament was that it was seriously questioned whether the Gospel of John fell into the same category as the Gospel of Thomas and Peter. Around 170 a group of Christians in Asia Minor known as the 'Alogi' rejected John's gospel as being the work of the Gnostic heretic, Cerinthus; and that was not the last objection. About fifty years later a priest in Rome called Gaius echoed their protest. But eventually four gospels, and only four, were recognized as authentic and authoritative.

Towards the end of the second century Irenaeus – a bishop in Gaul (France) who was familiar with the churches of Asia Minor and Rome – was explaining in his book *Against Heresies* why there obviously had to be four gospels. There were four regions of the world and four chief winds! At about the same time Tatian in Syria composed a harmony of the four gospels, the *Diatessaron*. (Only a fragment of this has survived, although it maintained itself as *the* gospel for the churches in Syria far into the fifth century.) After that, the signs of the authority of the four gospels in the whole Christian Church multiplied fast.

3

FOUR GOSPELS BY FOUR MEN

The oldest evidence about the origins of Mark's gospel comes from Bishop Papias. 'This also the elder used to say,' Papias recalled towards the end of the second century; almost certainly he meant John the Elder. 'Mark was the interpreter of Peter and wrote down accurately, but not in order, what he remembered of the things said or done by the Lord. He had neither heard the Lord nor followed him, but as I said had followed Peter. Peter adapted his teaching to meet people's needs, but not as though he was making a compilation of the sayings of the Lord; so that Mark made no mistake when writing down some things as he remembered them. He had only one intention: to omit nothing and to falsify nothing that he had heard.'

Bishop Eusebius, who preserved that fragment of the memories of Papias in his *Ecclesiastical History*, believed that Mark had written his gospel during Peter's lifetime before going to Alexandria to become its first bishop; but an altogether more likely account was provided by Bishop Irenaeus in his book *Against Heresies*. Irenaeus wrote at about the same date as Papias, more than a century before Eusebius.

He recalls that Peter's had been no ordinary death. Peter had been crucified when Paul (a Roman citizen) had been beheaded, in the course of the Emperor Nero's persecution of the Christians in Rome in (or about) the year 64. 'After their deaths,' Irenaeus adds, 'Mark, the disciple and interpreter of Peter, handed down to us in writing what Peter had proclaimed.' Although Irenaeus was familiar with the work of

Papias, we also know that he had been to Rome and took pride in his connection with the church there.

Many modern scholars agree that there is no good reason to reject such evidence about Mark's gospel, although the evidence dates from a century after the events. One reason for accepting it is that it would have been more impressive to assign the gospel to one of the apostles, for example to Peter himself, instead of to a man who had never been a disciple following Jesus. So almost certainly the author was John Mark, who features in the Acts of the Apostles – as the son of Mary in whose house in Jerusalem the Church had its first headquarters (12:12), and as the assistant of Barnabas and Paul in the mission to Cyprus (13:4-13). For some reason not explained, John Mark 'left them and went back to Jerusalem'; and Paul was very angry. We read in the account of Paul's second great missionary journey: 'Barnabas wanted to take John Mark with them, but Paul did not think it was right to take him, because he had not stayed with them to the end of their mission, but had turned back and left them in Pamphylia. They had a sharp argument between them, and separated from each other. Barnabas took Mark and sailed off to Cyprus . . .' (15:37-39).

Paul's letter to the Colossians from prison in Rome shows that he had been reconciled to Mark. 'Aristarchus, who is in prison with me, sends you greetings, and so does Mark, the cousin of Barnabas. You have already received instructions about him, to welcome him if he comes your way' (4:10). Paul's letter to Philemon (verse 24) names Mark as one of his fellow-workers. The Second Letter to Timothy says: 'Get Mark and bring him with you, because he can help me in the work' (4:11), and the First Letter of Peter refers

to 'my son Mark' (5:13). These two letters are thought
by many scholars to be the work of early Christians
not the apostles, but at least they show how strong
was the tradition that John Mark was a personal
assistant to Paul and Peter.

It does not follow that Mark had acquired Paul's
theological genius, or his eloquence in the presentation
of ideas. His command of a rough kind of Greek may
well have been better than Peter's, but his gospel con-
firms what Bishop Papias had heard: Mark never
received any orderly and comprehensive account of the
life of Jesus from Peter. The prominence of Peter in the
first chapter of the gospel, when he is called from his
fisherman's nets and when his mother-in-law is healed
in his home, is not maintained. On his next appearance
Peter is called 'Satan' despite his initiative in saying,
'You are the Messiah' (8:29, 33). Six days later Peter
shared a strange, mystical experience of Jesus (the
Transfiguration); but he was 'so frightened that he
did not know what to say' (9:6). In the final story,
Peter's cowardly part was such that in shame 'he
broke down and cried' (14:72). Mark may have
written such things about Peter with the reflection that
he himself had let Paul down in a crisis – and had never
fully understood him. Only one hero appears in his
gospel.

There may be a memory embodied in a little story
which otherwise seems pointless. It comes in the
account of the arrest of Jesus. 'A certain young man,
dressed only in a linen cloth, was following Jesus.
They tried to arrest him, but he ran away naked
leaving the linen cloth behind' (14:51, 52). This may
be John Mark's recollection of creeping out of his
home in his bedclothes, to watch the guests whose
supper in their large upstairs room had caused such

excitement – a memory, inserted to show that he, too, had once followed Jesus. It has also been suggested that John Mark may have been the man carrying a jar of water to show the disciples the way to the room (14:13, 14). A man doing a woman's work was the sign pre-arranged by Jesus, to ensure quiet for their supper. However, it is by no means certain that the Last Supper did take place in John Mark's home.

More to the point is the clear evidence of the gospel that when Mark wrote an hour of testing was upon his readers. Mark was doing more than to record a young man's memory when he put down the agonized prayer of Jesus in Gethsemane: 'Father! My Father! All things are possible for you. Take this cup away from me. But not what I want, but what you want' (14:36). The gospel is a call to be ready to share the cruel death which had destroyed all that was mortal of Jesus – and now of Peter and Paul also. Mark's is a gospel for martyrs. A climax comes when Peter has rebuked Jesus for speaking about being put to death. Jesus rebukes Peter: 'Get away from me, Satan. Your thoughts are men's thoughts, not God's!' Then Jesus calls the crowd with his disciples, and tells them: 'If anyone wants to come with me, he must forget himself, carry his cross, and follow me' (8:33, 34).

The whole gospel is a call to personal devotion. The first words spoken by Jesus in it are: 'Come with me' (1:17). The gospel is a call to humility. 'Whoever wants to be first must place himself last of all and be the servant of all' (9:35), and the message must be received with a childlike humility (10:15). The gospel is a call to a single-minded purity. 'If your hand makes you turn away, cut it off! It is better for you to enter life without a hand than to keep both hands and go off to hell, to the fire that never goes out' (9:43). The gospel

is a call to poverty. 'It is much harder for a rich
man to enter the Kingdom of God than for a camel to
go through the eye of a needle' – although those who
have left everything in order to follow Jesus are
promised compensations including eternal life – 'and
persecutions as well' (10:25-30). And the gospel is
a call to a courageous faith. 'If you do not doubt in
your heart, but believe that what you say will happen, it
will be done for you' (11:23).

Those who want to be with Jesus in his Kingdom
must drink his cup and be baptized in his way – which
means that they must suffer (10:35-45). 'You will
be arrested and taken to court. You will be beaten in
the synagogues; you will stand before rulers and kings
for my sake, to tell them the Good News . . . Men
will hand over their brothers to be put to death, and
fathers will do the same to their children; children will
turn against their parents and have them put to
death. Everyone will hate you because of me' (13:9-13).
The Lord who makes such promises arouses bewilderment and fear. 'Jesus was going ahead of the disciples,
who were filled with alarm; the people who followed
behind were afraid' (10:32). Modern scholars who
believe (as many do) that the gospel originally ended at
16:8 can point to the fact that the last words are
typical of the atmosphere: 'they were afraid'.

But 'this is the Good News about Jesus Christ, the
Son of God' (1:1)! The suffering prophesied by Jesus
for himself and his followers has a glorious ending, for
'whoever loses his life for me and the gospel will save
it' (8:35) and 'whoever holds out to the end will be
saved' (13:13). On the other hand, hell will be the
punishment of those who falter: 'there "their worms
never die, and the fire is never put out"' (9:46, 48).
And on earth the Jews who reject Jesus will experience

'trouble . . . far worse than any the world has ever known' (13:19). The prophecies of calamity for the temple and for Judea do not include descriptions of the fall of Jerusalem to the Romans in 70; Mark's gospel is therefore thought to have been written before that terrible event. But the fatal Jewish revolt against the Roman empire began in 66. Mark wrote at a time when his readers had to be warned against 'false Messiahs and false prophets' (13:22). One reason why this is Good News is that the other news is so bad.

Mark gives the Good News simply by announcing the victory of Jesus Christ over *evil* (in the shape of the demons who caused diseases), *sin* (in many shapes, beginning at 2:5), and finally *death* in the shape of hideous torture and execution, the worst punishment that the Romans could inflict.

He conceals nothing as he depicts the weakness of the human emotions of Jesus. 'Jesus was filled with pity' – but the Greek word may mean 'anger' (1:41). 'Jesus spoke harshly' (1:43). 'Jesus was angry' (3:5). Jesus was thought by people – it seems, including his own family – to have gone mad (3:21). Jesus was sleeping, and was woken up with the demand: 'Teacher, don't you care that we are about to die?' (4:38) Jesus was 'greatly surprised' at his rejection by his home town, where 'he was not able to perform any miracles', but the fact was that the people who had watched him as a boy and as a young man could say only, 'Isn't he the carpenter?' (6:1-6) Mark does not pretend that Jesus had all the answers. With a perfectly normal human ignorance Jesus had to ask a man his name (5:9), ask who had touched him (5:30), ask how much bread they had (8:5), and ask what they were arguing about (9:16). He did not know when the end of history would come (13:32). Jesus asked: 'Why do you call me

good? No one is good except God alone' (10:18). In
distress before his death, he told his friends: 'The
sorrow in my heart is so great that it almost crushes
me' – and he begged them to stay awake and give him
companionship (14:34). The dying words of Jesus
were: 'My God, my God, why did you abandon me?'
(15:34) But the victory over evil, sin, and death tells its
own story – that Jesus is the Son of God. Writing in the
style natural to him and his readers, Mark dramatizes
this story by giving the cries and screams of the
demons: 'You are God's holy messenger!' (1:24), 'You
are the Son of God!' (3:11)

Mark's gospel does not explain the mystery of
why the Son of God had to undergo such suffering, or
the mystery of why he was not acknowledged. As to the
first mystery, there are only hints of an explanation
when it is said that the death of Jesus will 'redeem
many people' or be a ransom liberating them from
slavery (10:45) and when at 14:24 there is a reference
to 'my blood which is poured out for many, my blood
which seals God's covenant' (or completes the new
agreement between God and his people). As to the
second mystery, the explanation is offered that Jesus
frequently ordered silence about his own status – silence
from the demons and even silence from the disciples
(8:30). According to Mark, it was only when Jesus
was solemnly and repeatedly questioned by the High
Priest that he made his claim publicly (14:61, 62).
But Mark gives no reason why Jesus had wanted such
silence.

Ever since William Wrede published a book on this
'Messianic secret' in Mark, in 1901, many scholars have
supplied the answer that in fact the historical Jesus
never claimed to be the Messiah, but that Mark shared
the faith of the Church in 65 that Jesus had been the

Messiah all along; therefore Mark had to do his best to explain why the claim was not more public. We shall discuss this possibility in the last chapter of this book. All that we need observe here is that mystery surrounds the Jesus of Mark. There seems to be no time for intellectual reflection; the pace is breathless. The mystery remains – but its practical consequences are not left at all obscure.

Mark's aim was to make the love and the demand of Jesus Christ so vivid that the persecuted Christians would feel themselves in the shoes of the rich man kneeling before Jesus on the road. 'Jesus looked straight at him with love and said, "You need only one thing. Go and sell all you have . . . then come and follow me" ' (10:21). For this purpose Mark became (so far as we know) the first man to write a gospel – because it seemed necessary to give more than a few sayings of Jesus, and when telling the story of Jesus it was necessary to tell of more than his last hours. He wanted to show how the teaching had expressed the life, and how the life had led up to the death. In his gospel, facing death gives the unity. The enemies of Jesus plan to kill him as early as 3:6. At the centre of the gospel lie three solemn prophecies of the Passion (8:31; 9:30, 31; 10:32-34).

Mark's use of the phrase 'the Good News' or 'the gospel' in his first sentence was the reason why the new kind of book that he invented came to be called by a new name: *a* gospel. Scholars suggest that there were three thoughts in the mind of Mark when he used the old phrase about *the* gospel. As one familiar with the Jewish scriptures since his boyhood, he would remember the Good News in chapters 40-55 of the prophetic Book of Isaiah. As one who had worked with Paul, he would remember that 'the Good News' had been one of that great man's favourite expressions. And as one who now lived in Rome, he would remember how often 'good news' was announced in the propaganda of the cult of the divine Emperor. So in Rome under Nero, he told the story of Jesus – the Messiah promised to Israel, the Son of God who had redeemed many people outside Israel, the King whose victory had come through endurance.

In his gospel a 'young man wearing a white robe' tells the women in the empty tomb of Jesus: 'Now go and give this message to his disciples, including Peter: "He is going to Galilee ahead of you; there you will see him, just as he told you" ' (16:7). Did Mark end by relating an appearance of the victorious Jesus to Peter in Galilee? If so, the ending has been lost. What we can be sure of is that Mark believed that Jesus Christ would show his victory to all who let him lead them into life and death.

Matthew

The fact that Mark's gospel was known to Matthew and Luke is some evidence of its spread far beyond Rome. But Matthew and Luke were both confident that they could do better. Perhaps Mark had done a hurried job in an emergency; anyway, Peter's reminiscences had not been orderly or complete. What was now needed was a comprehensive record of what Jesus had said and done, edited with an eye to a larger audience than Mark's.

Papias, as quoted by Eusebius, gives only one enigmatic sentence about Matthew. 'Matthew compiled the oracles in the Hebrew language, and each one interpreted them as best he could.' There is no doubt that this refers to Matthew, one of the twelve apostles. The doubt is what book is meant. Matthew's gospel is clearly *not* a translation into Greek from Hebrew. It seems therefore that, if the tradition known to Papias is correct, the apostle compiled either a collection of Old Testament prophecies, or a collection of sayings of Jesus, or some of the special material in this gospel – and the name of the man who interpreted these 'oracles' by writing the gospel is unknown. But in that case it remains a puzzle why the author of the gospel depended to such an extent on a non-disciple, Mark. Ninety per cent of Mark's gospel reappears with minor changes. Basically Matthew takes over Mark's framework. The explanation may be that the author of the gospel had as much respect for Peter's memories as for Matthew's. However, another possible explanation is that Papias has no real light to throw on how the gospel was written. And there is no second-century evidence apart from Papias.

It is therefore unsafe to interpret this gospel by concentrating on 'Matthew the tax collector' whose call by Jesus is described (9:9-13) – but who is called Levi by Mark and Luke. Fortunately, however, a good deal of the author's character shines through what he wrote. Half of his gospel is not in Mark, and of this half, a half is not in Luke either.

This quarter which is special to 'Matthew' (as the author will now be called) is distinctive enough. Its author is a Jew who is accurate about Jewish customs and does not explain them. He does not translate the Aramaic words which he includes at 5:22 (the Greek text has *Raca* where Today's English Version has 'You good-for-nothing!'), at 6:24 (the Greek has *mammon* where TEV has 'money'), and at 27:6 (the Greek has *korbanan* where TEV has 'blood-money'). He prefers the phrase 'Kingdom of heaven' (the Greek is plural – 'heavens') to 'Kingdom of God' because that is the reverent Jewish way to avoid speaking directly of God. He tends to write off foreigners. Food, drink, and clothes are 'the things the heathen are always concerned about' (6:32), and when a Christian refuses to listen to the Church about his sin, members of the Church are to treat him 'as though he were a foreigner or a tax collector' (18:17). But he is himself a Greek-speaking Jew, always using the Greek translation of the Old Testament, the Septuagint. As we have already noted, he quotes Isaiah 7:14 as 'the virgin will become pregnant', although the original Hebrew merely said 'the young woman' (1:23). His own Greek is far less clumsy than Mark's. And in his gospel come glimpses of the Christian mission to 'all peoples everywhere' (28:19). There is a hint of that in the initial story of visitors from the east (2:1-12). It has therefore been suggested that the author of this gospel was a Jewish rabbi who had become a Christian with a world-vision. If so, he has left a little portrait of himself in the saying of Jesus which he alone gives: 'Every teacher of the Law who becomes a disciple in the Kingdom of heaven is like a homeowner who takes new and old things out of his storage room' (13:52).

We do not know where the gospel was written; Syria seems the most likely place. But we can see fairly well the situation which made Matthew convinced that he had to expand Mark's gospel for the use of the Christians around him.

The rebellious Jerusalem fell to the Romans in the year 70, with scenes of horror which still sicken the reader of *The Jewish War* by Josephus. So the warning of Jesus came true: 'all who take the sword will die by the sword' (26:52). Matthew refers to this when he inserts into the parable of Jesus also given by Luke, the words: 'The King was very angry; he sent his soldiers, who killed those murderers and burned down their city' (22:7). But the fall of Jerusalem was not the end of the Jewish religion. On the contrary, many of the surviving rabbis gathered in the little town of Jamnia. In Jamnia or elsewhere during the next half-century, decisions were made that shaped the Judaism of the centuries to come. They agreed on the contents of the Old Testament in Hebrew and arranged for a more accurate translation into Greek. They began the massive writing down of the religious law which had previously been handed on by word of mouth. They did anything still needed to discredit and abolish the parties into which Judaism had previously been divided – the Sadducees who had conservatively supported the temple and who had accepted as authoritative only the first five books of the Old Testament; the Essenes who had rejected the temple and who had

C

developed their own exclusive sect; the excited readers and writers of 'apocalyptic' predictions of the imminent triumph of Israel. They regulated the worship which was to be carried on in the synagogues now that the temple was destroyed. They made it impossible for followers of Jesus of Nazareth to attend this worship by including among the 'Benedictions' recited in each synagogue every Sabbath these words: 'Let there be no hope for the traitors, and may the arrogant kingdom be rooted out soon in our days! May the Nazarenes and the heretics perish quickly and be blotted out from the Book of Life!' It was the triumph of the Pharisees on the ruins of the temple, and the transformation of Judaism confronted all Jews who had become Christians with a challenge no less grave than the crisis in Rome when Mark wrote.

Matthew, although writing before some of these developments, has to recognize that 'the Jews' now stand against the Christians. At one point he says that 'to this very day that is the report spread round by the Jews' (28:15). The situation after 70 colours references to the Jewish leadership in his gospel, including the terrible condemnations of the teachers of the Law and the Pharisees ('blind guides') which he has assembled in chapter 23. But his chief aim is positive. The very first sentence of his gospel announces where the true fulfilment of the Old Testament promises is to be found – in 'Jesus Christ, who was a descendant of David, who was a descendant of Abraham'. And he frequently insists that Jesus was a Jew, loyal to the meaning of the Old Testament. 'Do not think that I have come to do away with the Law of Moses and the teachings of the prophets. I have not come to do away with them, but to make their teachings come true. Remember this! As long as heaven and earth last, the least

point or the smallest detail of the Law will not be
done away with – not until the end of all things'
(5:17,18). Matthew expands Mark's gospel in order to
show more clearly that although most of the Jews have
now decisively rejected Jesus, the Christians (including
some converted Jews) rightly follow him – and are
therefore now God's people.

The 'Law of Moses' consisted of the Old Testament's
first five books. In Matthew's gospel there are therefore five principal collections of the sayings of Jesus.
Each collection ends with words such as 'Jesus
finished these things.' The first collection, the Sermon
on the Mount which might be called *The Law of the
Kingdom of Heaven*, ends at 7:28; the second collection (*Messengers of the Kingdom*) ends at 11:1; the
third (*Parables of the Kingdom*) ends at 13:53;
the fourth (*Servants of the Kingdom*) ends at 19:1;
and the fifth (*The Coming of the Kingdom*) ends at
26:1.

This message announces a radical novelty; and
although much of the Old Testament is upheld, Matthew
knows that he is reporting a revolution. He alone gives
the little parable comparing the impact of the message to
the discovery of treasure hidden in a field, or an
unusually fine pearl hidden among the merchant's
inferior stock. The only sensible investment is to
sell everything one has in order to buy the field or the
pearl (13:44-46). Matthew does not see with a complete clarity what is old and what is new in the
message. At times he sounds like a conservative.
But six times in chapter 5 he hears the voice of Jesus
commanding a revolutionary simplicity. 'You have
heard that men were told in the past . . . But now I tell
you . . .'

We may vaguely imagine that in Matthew's gospel the

Sermon on the Mount is delivered to all and sundry. In fact the teaching is given to 'the disciples' gathered round Jesus up a hill away from the great crowds (5:1). The Sermon is therefore a kind of law for the new community of Christians. The old people of God consisted of the twelve tribes of Israel. Already Mark had implied that Jesus was founding a new and purer Israel when he had listed the twelve apostles (3:13-19). But Matthew assembled for these twelve (in chapter 10) more elaborate instructions than any found in Mark, and he called the community resulting from their mission 'the Church' – a word which does not occur elsewhere in our gospels. (In Greek it is *ekklesia*, and in the Greek Old Testament that word is used for the assembly of Israel.) The community is to have law-givers. Peter is told: 'On this rock foundation I will build my church, which not even death will ever be able to overcome. I will give you the keys of the Kingdom of heaven; . . . what you permit on earth will be permitted in heaven' (16:18,19). The authorization is extended to all the other disciples at 18:18.

It is to be a community inspired by the vision of God's holiness. The Sermon on the Mount has the theme: 'You must be perfect – just as your father in heaven is perfect' (5:48). There is also a down-to-earth insistence on good personal relations, which if need be should be regulated by the Church (18:15-17). There are instructions about fasting (6:16-18), although Matthew has taken on from Mark the historical fact that the disciples of Jesus did not fast (9:14). If this community remains united and faithful, it will be rewarded. 'Whenever two of you on earth agree about anything you pray for, it will be done for you by my Father in heaven. For where two or three come together in my name, I am there with them' (18:19) – 'always'

(28:20). At the last judgement, the weed-like evildoers
will be burned but 'God's people will shine like the
sun in their Father's Kingdom' (13:43). In another
parable which only Matthew gives, all who have
befriended the disciples are rewarded with the words of
the King: 'Whenever you did this for one of the
least important of these brothers of mine, you did it for
me!' (25:40) In other words, 'whoever gives even
a drink of cold water to one of the least of these my
followers, because he is my follower, will certainly
receive his reward' (10:42).

In Matthew's gospel Jesus demonstrates his authority
by miracles (there are ten miracles after the Sermon
on the Mount) and he accepts the worship he arouses,
as when he walks on the water and the disciples
exclaim: 'Truly you are the Son of God!' (14:33)
Matthew tones down many of Mark's references to the
humanity of Jesus, and adds highly dramatic miracles
or promises of them. Examples are the coin worth
enough for the temple tax, to be found in the mouth of
the first fish Peter catches (17:24-27); and the resurrection of 'many of God's people' in the earthquake on the
first Good Friday (27:52,53). But it is fair to say
about the Jesus presented by Matthew that his chief
claim and his chief success are *moral*, in accordance
with the highest tradition of the Old Testament.
Matthew gives this key comment before any of the
great miracles: 'The crowd was amazed at the way he
taught. He wasn't like their teachers of the Law; instead,
he taught with authority' (7:28,29).

It is also fair to add that the Jesus presented
by Matthew is not a ruthless dictator. Matthew was
writing for people who were tired of being pushed
around. They were for the most part poor people, and
they were the adherents of a religion under attack both

from Romans and from Jews. They needed to be reminded that Jesus was not a terrible law-giver and punishment-giver but a gentle teacher of heavenly wisdom, tender to the needs of his hearers. In Matthew's special material we read the moving words: 'Come to me, all of you who are tired from carrying your heavy loads, and I will give you rest. Take my yoke and put it on you, and learn from me, because I am gentle and humble in spirit; and you will find rest. The yoke I will give you is easy, and the load I will put on you is light' (11:28-30).

The moral – rather than the miraculous – authority of the Jesus it presented was, it seems, the main reason why Matthew's gospel won so much respect in the next two centuries. All the evidence surviving from that time suggests that the Christians largely lacked the profound insights of Paul and the intense vision of Mark. But in the long battle against the hostility of the Roman empire, the Church's chief weapon was its moral purity – never complete, but sufficiently undeniable to answer the various slanders that circulated. Matthew's gospel suited this mood perfectly, long after the crisis of the fall of Jerusalem and the rise of the new Judaism. Its instructions to collaborate with the Romans (5:41, etc.) were no doubt influential in persuading the Christians in Palestine and Syria to abstain completely from the last Jewish revolt, under Bar Cochba in 126. (We are told that the Christians did abstain, and many of them were slaughtered by the rebels.) But in the long run, that did not matter greatly. The numbers of Christians who were acutely conscious that they were also Jews declined. The centre of the religion shifted for ever from Palestine and Syria, and something happened which no one had expected in the days of the historical Jesus or in the next forty years:

Christianity became almost entirely a Gentile affair. Matthew's gospel could not now command respect chiefly by its presentation of the Church as the new Israel. We have to think of the permanent moral authority of this Jesus if we are to learn why in Gentile congregations throughout the Roman empire Matthew's became the most honoured gospel.

When the persecutions ceased and the Church became free to order its worship in public, this was the gospel most read at the Holy Communion Sunday by Sunday. And in later times, when the Roman empire was itself scarcely remembered, even people who rejected all miracles, and all the doctrines and worship of the Church, would still find the essence of Christianity in the Sermon on the Mount.

Luke

Less need be said here about the Gospel of Luke. It forms a unity with the Acts of the Apostles, which has already been introduced in Today's English Version (David L. Edwards, *Good News in Acts*, 1975). In any case, the main purpose of Luke's gospel is immediately clear if it is read together with Acts. The aim is to present the Jesus about whom old Simeon speaks in thanksgiving to God in the Jerusalem temple:

'A light to reveal your way to the Gentiles,
    and bring glory to your people Israel' (2:32).

Many of the differences between this gospel and the other Synoptics emphasize that this author is not a Jew. He pays less attention than Matthew or Mark to controversies about Jewish laws and customs. He is vague about the geography of Palestine. For example, he writes: 'As Jesus made his way to Jerusalem he went between Samaria and Galilee (17:11)! What really interests him is that the way to Jerusalem will lead 'to all nations, beginning in Jerusalem' (24:47). As early as 9:51, Jesus 'made up his mind and set out on his way to Jerusalem'. Everything between that point and 19:45 takes place on the road to Jerusalem, and to stress this theme Jesus says at 13:33: 'I must be on my way today, tomorrow, and the next day; it is not right for a prophet to be killed anywhere except in Jerusalem.' After the crucifixion, the journey is resumed. 'Jesus himself drew near and walked along with them' – to Emmaus and to the world (24:15).

Luke's gospel has an atmosphere different from Mark's message to the persecuted. Like Acts, it is dedicated to 'Theophilus' – a name which means 'Lover of God'. Theophilus may be an imaginary reader representing the Gentile world, or he may be a highly placed Roman able to act as patron to this book. Luke is the only contributor to the New Testament who mentions the name of a Roman emperor. He adds a list of local rulers (3:1,2), and the mention of many friendly (or at least just) officials in Acts reinforces our impression that Luke is anxious to show that the patronage of officials can greatly assist the progress of the cause of the Lord of lords. At the very beginning of his public work, the Jesus of Luke openly claims that it is the work of the Messiah. He reads from the scroll in the synagogue at Nazareth:

'The Spirit of the Lord is upon me,
    because he has chosen me to preach the Good News
      to the poor.
He has sent me to proclaim liberty to the captives,
    and recovery of sight to the blind;
to set free the oppressed,
    and announce the year when the Lord will save his
      people.'

The reader's next words detonate like a bomb: 'This passage of scripture has come true today, as you heard it being read' (4:16-21). As early as 5:8 Jesus is called 'Lord' by Peter; and often in the gospel he is referred to simply as 'the Lord', in accordance with the practice in the Gentile churches in the second half of the first century. He dies with confident words: 'Father! In your hands I place my spirit!' (23:46) He rises to lead his followers forward in peace, joy, wonder, and thanksgiving (24:36-53).

The atmosphere in this gospel is also different from that in Matthew's. To be sure, Jerusalem has fallen. The Jesus of Luke foresees this: 'The days will come upon you when your enemies will surround you with barricades, blockade you, and close in on you from every side. They will completely destroy you and the people within your walls; not a single stone will they leave in its place, because you did not recognize the time when God came to save you!' (19:43,44) 'The days are coming when people will say, "How lucky are the women who never had children . . ." ' (23:29) But Luke's gospel and Acts do not put the fall of Jerusalem at the centre of their picture of history. In the gospel Christians are told to be ready for whatever comes – 'because the Son of Man will come at an hour when you are not expecting him' (12:35-40). Meanwhile Luke sees that God himself is patient, like the gardener who spares an unfruitful fig tree for another year (16:6-9). In his two volumes Luke concentrates on the mission of the Church as history goes on. This mission involves far more missionaries than the original twelve – a point already made in Luke's special material about the mission of 'another seventy-two men' (10:1-12, 17-20). At the end of the Acts of the Apostles, Paul tells the Jews in Rome: 'God's message of salvation has been sent to the Gentiles. They will listen!' (28:28) But the same point is made by Jesus in his inaugural sermon at Nazareth, when he observes that Elijah and Elisha were sent to foreigners not Jews (4:25-27). The horizon of this gospel stretches far beyond Palestine.

This atmosphere suggests a date when the Church has responded to the call to preach to the world – but has not yet been plunged into the persecution under the Emperor Domitian. There seems no good reason to reject the tradition (which we find in the Muratorian Canon towards the end of the second century) that Luke was the author both of this gospel and of Acts. This would be 'Luke, our dear doctor' mentioned in Paul's letter to the Colossians (4:14). On the whole, the suggestion that Luke wrote the passages in Acts which refer to 'us' fits in with the evidence, and so does the suggestion that the author of those passages wrote the rest of Acts and the gospel too. These are problems which scholars are right to discuss, but none disproves Luke's authorship. The main difficulties come from the author's lack of knowledge both of the facts and of the theology contained in Paul's letters, but these difficulties are not insuperable if we picture Luke writing some fifteen years after Paul's death, without access to the letters (which had not yet been collected) – writing as a superb artist in words rather than as a meticulously exact historian, and writing as a doctor rather than as an abstract thinker.

The character of the author is clear enough in his choice of material for his gospel. Three-fifths of it does not come from Mark, and a third has no parallel in Matthew. Most of Luke's own material is found in the section from 9:51 to 18:14, where nothing appears from Mark. Curiously, no use is made anywhere of Mark 6:45-8:26, which has led to suggestions that this part may have been missing from the copy of Mark available to Luke.

Luke's sympathy with foreigners comes out in his attitude to the Samaritans, who because of their mixed blood were despised by the Jews. In Luke's own material, Jesus refuses to call down fire from heaven on a Samaritan village (9:51-55); he praises a good Samaritan above a priest and a temple assistant (10:25-37); he is moved because while nine Jews are forgetful, a Samaritan who has been healed returns to give thanks (17:11-19).

Luke's sympathy with women – at a time when every Jewish man was told to thank God daily that he had not been born a woman – is shown in his stories of

Elizabeth the mother of John the Baptist and Mary the
mother of Jesus (1:23-2:7); the widow of Nain whose
only son was dead (7:11-17); the woman 'who lived a
sinful life' but showed 'great love' to Jesus by bathing
his feet with tears and perfume (7:36-48); the many
women 'who used their own resources to help Jesus
and his disciples' (8:1-3); Martha and Mary in their
home (10:38-42); the woman crippled for eighteen
years (13:10-17).

Luke respects those who are 'faithful in handling
worldly wealth' (16:1-13), but he is far from being a
snob. He rejoices that the poor will be lifted up and the
hungry filled. That is what the mother of Jesus sings
(1:46-55); that is what Jesus himself says (6:20,21).
Luke's special material includes a parable warning
those who 'pile up riches for themselves but are not
rich in God's sight' (12:13-21); advice to sit in the
lowest place at a feast, for 'everyone who makes
himself great will be humbled, and everyone who
humbles himself will be made great' (14:7-11); and
an order to be hospitable to 'the poor, the crippled, the
lame, and the blind' (14:12-14). Luke alone gives the
parable which contrasts the poor man, Lazarus, with
the rich man who is in hell (16:19-31).

Above all, Luke praises those who are humble
before God – the obscure but devout and patiently
expectant Jews who fill his first two chapters; the
disciples who say, 'we are ordinary servants – we have
only done our duty' (17:7-10); the worshippers who
persevere in prayer like a widow badgering a corrupt
judge (18:1-8); the humble people who secretly
pray, 'God, have pity on me, a sinner!' (18:9-14)
Among Christians, 'the greatest one among you must
be like the youngest, and the leader must be like the
servant' (22:26).

Luke's gospel moves into the world. But the Lord who leads attracts his followers one by one. He draws them by loving them and by being 'among you as one who serves' (22:27). The little tax collector up the tree is spotted: 'Hurry down, Zacchaeus!' (19:1-9) The criminal on the cross is told: 'today you will be in Paradise with me' (23:43). This is the gospel of the one lost coin and the one lost son, now the cause of the music and the dancing (15:8-32). So the Christmas angels celebrate because peace has come to the humble folk with whom God is pleased (2:14).

John

When we come to the fourth gospel, we move into a different world. It is possible that John wrote without any knowledge of the gospels of Mark, Matthew, and Luke. This may not seem probable, but nothing in his gospel proves that John used the other three.

We move into a world where there is no trace of Jesus making a secret of his Messiahship, as he does in Mark's gospel where he refuses to say 'by what right I do these things' (11:33). Instead, the Jesus of John declares: 'You will die in your sins if you do not believe that "I Am Who I Am"' (8:24) – and he openly challenges the religious authorities by cleansing the temple at the beginning of his work (2:13-21). Even if Today's English Version goes too far in putting quotation marks around 'I am . . .' (thus making it an explicit reference to God's self-disclosure in Exodus 3:14), the contrast between Mark and John is still striking.

There is little teaching of the kind assembled by Matthew in the Sermon on the Mount; instead, the Jesus of John teaches about himself, his union with God and the disciples' union with him. There are many fewer human details and many fewer parables than in Luke's gospel; instead, we read long speeches varied by spectacular miracles. We have seen that each of the other gospel-writers has a tendency shown by his choice of material, but that the other three do not stress their own teaching in their own words. In John's gospel we are often at a loss to know whether we are reading the words of Jesus or of John – as may be seen by any reader of (for example) the conversation with Nicodemus in chapter 3.

3. the Christ is the agent of a new Creation (chs 1-2)

He is the life of the world (chs 3-6)

Light of the world (chs 7-9)

Rejected by his own people (chs 10-12)

But acknowledged by all who believe in him (chs 13-20)

Prologue Hymn —

No other gospel in the New Testament has aroused such uncertainty about who wrote it and what he intended. We have already noticed that there was a good deal of hesitation before this gospel was included with the others in the New Testament, but these early doubts were as nothing in comparison with the heat of the modern debate about the authorship and purpose. This uncertainty is ironic, because the gospel says who wrote it and what he wanted. We read at 21:24 that the 'other disciple, whom Jesus loved', is the man 'who spoke of these things, the one who also wrote them down; and we know that what he said is true.' And we read at 20:31 that these 'mighty' works have been written down in this book 'that you may believe that Jesus is the Messiah, the Son of God, and that through this faith you may have life in his name.'

The statement about the authorship comes in a chapter which seems to have been added as an epilogue when the gospel had already been completed by the climax just quoted (20:31). It declares that the group publishing chapter 21 can vouch for the truth of what has been said. Since the language of this last chapter shows no remarkable difference from the rest of the gospel, the implication may well be that the group has in some way edited the whole. At 19:35 there is a similar certificate that 'the one who saw this happen has spoken of it.'

But who was the disciple who 'spoke of these things'? He appears at 13:23, close to Jesus at the Last Supper; at 19:26, close to Jesus on his cross; at 20:2, with Simon Peter on the first Easter morning; and finally at 21:20, with Simon Peter when they meet the risen Jesus by the lake in Galilee. He may also be meant when 'another disciple' is mentioned as being

well known to the High Priest and as introducing
Simon Peter into the courtyard of the High Priest's
house (18:15, 16). The belief that he was John the son
of Zebedee depends not on this gospel but on the
fact that the other gospels often group Peter, James,
and John as the three intimates of Jesus who share
some of his most private experiences. (James is
ruled out as the beloved disciple because he was
martyred long before the fourth gospel was written:
Acts 12:2.) There is also support from the Church's
tradition. Irenaeus (about 180) wrote: 'John, the
disciple of the Lord, who had leaned upon his breast,
published his gospel while he was living at Ephesus in
Asia.' The Muratorian Canon (of about the same
date) ascribes the gospel to 'John, one of the disciples'.

The concluding statement of the gospel's purpose is
frank about the intention 'that you may believe'
– compared with the declared aim of Luke 'that you
will know the full truth of all those matters which you
have been taught' by means of an 'orderly account' of
'the things that have taken place among us' (1:1-4).
We have already seen that Mark, Matthew, and Luke
all had purposes which were religious rather than
strictly historical, but this motive is even stronger in
John.

To him, the truth is such that a man knows when he
has been spiritually reborn (3:3-8). It is what makes a
man free (8:31-2). *It is Jesus* – who is 'the way, the
truth, and the life' (14:6). The fourth gospel therefore
ignores many events which to its author do not
particularly reveal this truth. One trouble is that
these events include those in which according to the
Synoptic gospels John the son of Zebedee was most
memorably involved: his call while fishing, his inclusion in the twelve apostles, the transfiguration of

Jesus, the request of his mother for a place next to the throne of Jesus in the glorious Kingdom, his presence close to the anguished prayer in Gethsemane. This gospel is silent about all these things, and it never mentions John's brother James. It says very little about Galilee; everything after 7:10 takes place in Jerusalem. It is not at all what we should expect as the memoirs of the apostle John.

The authorship remains a riddle. If the author was John the son of Zebedee, he had no intention of recalling his experience in any detail. If he was another disciple, his identity is unknown. Perhaps he was John the Elder, whom Papias mentioned in addition to John the apostle (see page 50). Another possibility is that the 'we' mentioned at 21:24 created most of the gospel, using only a few memories from an eyewitness. Or the gospel may embody the traditions of a worshipping Christian congregation.

We are left not with knowledge of the author but with the gospel itself – and with its claim to give knowledge of the 'truth' of Jesus. The intensive modern study of the gospel has included the recognition by many scholars (notably by C. H. Dodd) that it incorporates some material with as good a claim to be historical truth as anything in the Synoptic gospels. At important points, this fourth gospel seems to be the most accurate. For example, John states that Jesus died on the day before the Passover feast (13:1, 19:31). This may be compared with the report of the other gospels that he died on the actual day of the feast, a very extraordinary day for an arrest, trial, and execution.

John also states that during the public work of Jesus two other Passovers occurred (2:13, 6:4) – which may be compared with the impression left by the other gospels that the public work took only one year, leading

up to the single Passover. (The only other indications of
time in Mark's gospel are the ripening wheat harvest
at 2:23 and the green grass at 6:39 – signs of spring in
Palestine.) John tells of three visits by Jesus to Judea
and Jerusalem, the final one lasting for about half a
year – which may be compared with the failure of the
other gospels to explain why the city was so intensely
interested in a Galilean. And John informs us that the
first disciples of Jesus were recruited from among
the disciples of John the Baptist (1:33-42) – which
may be compared with the failure of the other gospels to
explain why fishermen should respond to a preacher
who suddenly appeared and told them to leave everything. On all these historical questions, it may well
be John who is right.

But early in the second century Clement the scholar
of Alexandria was already describing John's as 'a
spiritual gospel', and there can be no doubt that it
was intended chiefly to convey spiritual knowledge.
It does this partly by telling of seven 'mighty works'.
John's comment on the first applies to them all: 'he
revealed his glory, and his disciples believed in him.'
These mighty works are: the turning of water into
wine at Cana – Jesus brings joy (2:1-12); the healing of
the official's son – Jesus gives life by his words
(4:43-54); the healing at the pool – Jesus frees from the
paralysis of sin (5:1-18; 7:21-31); the feeding of
the thousands – Jesus is the bread that God gives so
that the world may truly live (6:1-59); the healing of
the man born blind – Jesus has come so that the blind
should see and that those who 'see' should be shown up
as blind (9:1-41); the raising of Lazarus – whoever
believes in Jesus will never really die (11:1-44); the
'lifting up' and the glory of the cross and resurrection of

Jesus himself, drawing all men (12:20-50 interprets all that follows).

The spiritual knowledge which the disciples can gain from these 'mighty works' is explained to them in the speeches of Jesus as given by John. These speeches are far removed from the conversations in, say, Mark's gospel. A typical passage occurs in chapter 4 of John's gospel. Jesus sits by the well 'tired out by the journey'. But his talk with the woman of Samaria leads quickly from a request for a drink to profound religious truth, and when the disciples return with food, begging Jesus 'Teacher, have something to eat!', he answers: 'I have food to eat that you know nothing about . . . to obey the will of him who sent me and finish the work he gave me to do.' In these speeches, Jesus declares that he is 'the Son of Man, who came down from heaven' (3:13); the Messiah (4:26); the Son of God (5:19); the bread of life (6:35); the light of the world (8:12); the eternal 'I am' before Abraham was born (8:58); the good shepherd, willing to die for the sheep (10:11); one with the Father (10:30); the resurrection and the life (11:25); the making visible of the Father (12:45; 14:9); the conqueror of the world (16:33). Finally Jesus prays at length for the unity and glory of the disciples and of 'those who believe in me because of their message' (17:1-26).

It is impossible *both* to accept that the Synoptic gospels give broadly a reliable account of the shape of events in the life of Jesus *and* to accept that Jesus so openly performed such miracles and so explicitly made such superhuman claims about himself. We must choose, and the conclusion of almost all who have studied and pondered the matter with a modern honesty is that we cannot always rely on the mighty works or the

speeches in John as historical evidence, although they
include some straightforward history. Instead, most
modern scholars would say that the 'mighty works' of
Jesus in the fourth gospel are to be regarded chiefly as
dramas to show the glory of Jesus, and the speeches of
Jesus in the fourth gospel are to be read mainly as
speeches in those great dramas, communicating a very
deep understanding of who Jesus is in eternal reality.

It has often been asked: was John a Greek or a
Jew, and did he write for the Church or for the world?
But John's gospel refuses to be put into any of these
categories.

The fact that John began with the 'Word' (in Greek
Logos) in his prologue shows that he wrote for fairly
well educated people familiar with the phrase and with
the philosophy in its background. The idea of the
Word of God giving shape to all creation – the source of
life, the light shining on all men – was an idea popular
with many reflective and religiously minded people in
the first century. To Gentiles such as the Stoic philo-
sophers and their pupils, it was the Reason, Vitality,
and Order in all things: it was what made the universe
which rational men could contemplate. To Greek-
speaking Jews such as Philo of Alexandria it was the
equivalent of the Wisdom of God in the Old Testament.
John's audience included Gentiles who needed the
elementary information that *Rabbi* meant 'Teacher' and
Messiah meant 'Christ' (1:38, 41), and that the Passover was a Jewish feast (2:13) – but his language would
be familiar to Greek-speaking Jews. Much of it was
familiar in Palestine. For example, the contrast between
the Sons of Light and the Sons of Darkness occurs
prominently in the scrolls left by the Essene monks of
Qumran. And John's own thought is thoroughly Jewish.
His mind is saturated with meditation on the Old

Testament. He broods over the mystery: why have most of the Jews rejected Jesus?

This gospel is a profound statement of the Christian's union with Christ in the Church. It does not discuss the compassion which a Jew should show for a Samaritan. Indeed, it shows little compassion to the Jews. To them, it says: 'You are the children of your father, the Devil' (8:44). What it shows is the love of a Christian for his fellow-Christians and his Lord – a love which responds to the love of Jesus.

Jesus, John proclaims, 'had always loved those who were his own in the world, and he loved them to the very end' (13:1). So chapters 13, 14, 15, 16, and 17 move from one exultant affirmation to another about what Jesus does for Christians. He makes them clean, he sets them an example of humility towards each other, he gives them his new commandment to love one another, he prepares a place for them in heaven, he shows them the Father, he enables them to do greater works than his own, he does whatever they ask for in his name, he sends the Spirit of truth to stay with them for ever, he teaches them everything, he gives them his own peace, he remains united with them as a vine is united with its branches, he calls them his friends, he has chosen them so that they no longer belong to the world, he fills them with the kind of gladness no one can take away from them, he gives them a unity as close as his own union with his Father, he protects them so that not one of them is lost, he puts his joy in their hearts in all its fullness, he keeps them safe from the Evil One, he gives them the glory which his Father gave him, he lives in them with the love which his Father has for him.

Yet John also wrote for Greeks such as those who in his gospel 'came to Philip . . . and said "Sir, we want to see Jesus" ' (12:21). He wrote in order to show that the meaning of Jesus was universal and could satisfy the deepest hungers of the spirit of man. He did not conceal the use made by Jesus of Jewish terms such as the 'Kingdom of God' or the 'Son of Man', or the place in Christianity of the Jewish expectation of the last judgement when the righteous will 'rise to life on the last day' (11:24). But his message was phrased in such a way that all thinking people of his generation could begin to understand. It was a demand for personal faith, and it promised that the believer would rise to eternal life here and now, for 'this *is* eternal life: for men to know . . . the only true God, and to know Jesus Christ' (17:3).

John is a magnificent witness to what was believed about Jesus some sixty years after his crucifixion. And he is a witness who has not been captured by mythology. His gospel is greater than history, but does not ignore it – 'the Word became a human being and lived among us' (1:14). It is greater than morality, but does not contradict it – 'as I have loved you, so you must love one another' (13:34).

4

THE HISTORICAL JESUS

We have looked at Jesus through the eyes of Christians in the second half of the first century – particularly through the eyes of the four men who wrote the gospels collected by the Church in the New Testament. It may seem that in our quest for truth we cannot honestly go any further; for it may seem that we have come to the end of the facts. But that is not the case.

The gospels are indeed like portraits painted by artists who interpret the character of their subject with their own concerns, their own insights, and their own styles. But it does *not* follow that we can never know anything about how the man himself really looked. On the contrary, we can know a great deal. The modern study of Jesus, using historical methods only, can be taken further. It is like comparing a series of portraits with each other and with anything else available about the subject and his background. Sometimes one has to strip the varnish away to reveal the original colour; at other times one has to resist the temptation to believe that just because a feature appears in a portrait it cannot be true to life. Sometimes one uses a magnifying glass on a detail; at other times one stands back and looks at all the material as a whole. What results is not an accurate photograph. But it does give the outline of the face of a man.

In this chapter we shall sum up the solid results of the quest of the historical Jesus. We shall put down facts which almost all scholars nowadays accept as being facts, as a result of the international discussion over two centuries. We shall record these facts by making ten very short statements and adding a few quite so non-controversial as the statements which they follow. But they will state positions which few serious scholars reject, and when they appeal to the gospels they will do so in a way which most scholars accept.

1. Jesus was crucified as a suspected rebel under Pontius Pilate, who was governor of Judea from 26 to 36.

It is impossible that all the varied writing about Jesus which we have been considering in this book should refer to a man who never existed. It is equally impossible that the Christians should have invented the fact that he was executed as a criminal by crucifixion – for 'Christ on the cross' was an almost insuperable obstacle in their evangelism.

Crucifixion was a Roman punishment administered only for the most serious crimes by slaves and people of low class. Many suggestions have been made since the days of Reimarus that Jesus was a political leader, in which case Pilate was right to have him executed as a rebel or potential rebel, alongside 'two bandits' (Mark 15:27). But the only evidence which we possess suggests that Jesus and his movement avoided identification with the many rebellions or rebellious plots of the time. Paul told the Christians in Rome that the Emperor Nero, who was soon to have him executed, was 'God's servant working for your own good', so that obedience, honour, and taxes were due to the political authorities 'as a matter of conscience' (13:1-7). We are told that the Christians in Palestine dissociated themselves from the great rebellions of 66 and 126.

Those who wish to present Jesus as a rebel naturally claim that all this was a later Christian attempt to gloss over the revolutionary origins of the movement.

They cite the inclusion of Simon the Zealot (in Today's English Version 'Simon the Patriot') among the twelve apostles. It is also possible that Judas Iscariot came from the Zealots who were (or supported) guerrillas or 'freedom fighters', since his second name may come from the Latin *sicarius* or 'dagger man'. Certainly Jesus was surrounded by such men. Galilee was full of them, and some 'rebels who had committed murder in the riot' were in prison in Jerusalem (Mark 15:7). It is reasonable to suppose that he attracted some of them as a potential figurehead. Luke may well be referring to political hopes of liberation when he has the disciples say sadly: 'We had hoped that he would be the one who was going to redeem Israel!' (24:21) John may well be right in saying that on at least one occasion, when the thousands had eaten together in an atmosphere of great excitement, 'they were about to come and get him, to make him king by force' (6:15). And certainly the enthusiasm of the triumphant entry into Jerusalem was enough to alarm the police. Mark says that it was a demonstration chanting: 'Praise God! God bless him who comes in the name of the Lord! God bless the coming kingdom of our father David! Praise be to God!' (11:9, 10) Luke's report of the shouts would be even more alarming: 'God bless the king who comes in the name of the Lord! Peace in heaven, and glory to God!' (19:38)

But against this must be balanced the strong evidence that Jesus made a special point of befriending tax collectors and advocated the payment of taxes to the Roman Emperor (Mark 12:13-17). Equally strong is the evidence in Q that Jesus admired a Roman officer's sense of discipline. Jesus is said to have declared that men of such quality would feast with Abraham, Isaac, and Jacob – a compliment which not many Christians would have paid to the Roman army (Matthew 8:5-13). He is also reported as urging a people which seethed with rebellion: 'If one of the occupation troops forces you to carry his pack one mile, carry it another mile' (Matthew 5:41). Luke's whole aim in his gospel and Acts was to commend the story of Jesus to Theophilus and to the Roman empire in general, and many passages included by him echo his angels in affirming that the Christian message brought 'peace on earth' (2:14).

There is a curious incident in Luke's gospel (22:35-38). At their last supper with him, the disciples are advised by Jesus that 'whoever does not have a sword must sell his coat and buy one' – and two then say that they already wear swords (as most men did when travelling or in a strange city). Jesus comments, 'That is enough!' But Luke also reports that when arrested Jesus stopped the use of these swords when one had cut off the right ear of the High Priest's slave: 'Enough of this!' (22:47-51) And it seems that the first piece of advice is meant to be ironic, in keeping with the Old Testament reference that Jesus is now quoted as making: 'He was included with the criminals.' If he did not understand the mention of swords as ironic, Luke would surely not have added it to the material he took over from Mark.

The evidence is that when challenged, Jesus could only affirm that yes – there *was* a sense in which he claimed to be King of the Jews. But if Mark is right to report that Jesus begged people not to call him Messiah in public, the historical explanation seems to be that Jesus was well aware of how dangerous any use of the title was. Its widespread use (as in the demonstration at the entry into Jerusalem) would quickly lead to the end of his mission. Unless he raised the standard of revolt and triumphed as a rebel against the Roman army, he would be handed over to the authorities and under Roman colonialism could expect only one fate. However, we are justified by the evidence in saying that Pilate was wrong to include Jesus among the criminals such as the bandits crucified with him. For Jesus was no rebel.

We do not know for certain *when* Jesus 'suffered under Pontius Pilate'.

Another Roman official, Gallio, is mentioned in the Acts of the Apostles (18:12-17) and an inscription carved at the time shows that the date was 51; the evidence which we have in the New Testament indicates that about twenty years before that, Saul of Tarsus became convinced that Jesus of Nazareth was alive although he had been crucified. Luke (3:1) records the tradition that John the Baptist began preaching 'in the fifteenth year of the rule of Emperor Tiberius'; this year began officially on 19 August 28, although some evidence suggests that the year was reckoned from the previous autumn in the Eastern parts of the empire. If John is right to say that Jesus was crucified in a year when the Passover feast took place on a Sabbath (Saturday), that means it was 30 or 33. John dates the cleansing of the temple by Jesus at the beginning of his public work in the year 27-28 (2:20). Therefore according to the fourth gospel, Jesus died on 7 April 30. But we have already shown how difficult it is to rely on John for historical facts. This is the only evidence we have about the dating of what many regard as the turning point of the world's history.

In the sixth century the monk Dionysius suggested that all years should be dated either 'Before Christ' or *Anno Domini*. But if Matthew is right that Herod the Great was alive when Jesus was born (2:1-21), that

means that Jesus was born before 4 BC. Luke also says
that Herod was King (1:5), but adds that the birth took
place in the year of the 'first census' when Quirinius
was governor of Syria (2:2). The only such census
known to us took place in AD 6. It sparked off a
revolt which was put down with many crucifixions in
Galilee; this is referred to in Acts (5:37). It is not
absolutely impossible that P. Sulpicius Quirinius, who
is known to have been in the Roman colonial ad-
ministration then, organized an enrolment in the
kingdom of Herod the Great, but it does not seem very
likely. Certainly there is no evidence to support Luke in
believing that 'Emperor Augustus sent out an order for
all the citizens of the Empire to register themselves
for the census' (2:1).

It seems, therefore, that we have no reliable information about when Jesus was born, except that
during his public work he was 'about thirty years old'
(Luke 3:23), 'not even fifty years old' (John 8:57).

2. *Although he identified himself with the holiness
movement around John the Baptist, Jesus claimed that
a greater and more joyful event was taking place around
him.*

The work of John the Baptist, summoning Jews to
repentance and to a greater holiness of life, is mentioned by the historian Josephus. In the Acts of the
Apostles there is a report that in Alexandria about the
year 50 there were still Jews who 'knew only the baptism
of John' (18:25). But the main evidence for the
impact made by the Baptist comes from the four gospels
– which state that the Son of God, the Saviour, was
himself baptized by John in the river Jordan. To
admit that Jesus submitted himself to an act which
so obviously symbolized the washing away of sin was

embarrassing. In John's gospel this embarrassment is put into the mouth of the Baptist himself, who is re-assured by the voice of God (1:19-34). In Matthew's gospel the Baptist says: 'I ought to be baptized by you' (3:14). But at least the act showed that Jesus identified himself with his people. He did not come as a bolt from the blue.

The evidence also suggests that in some sense Jesus belonged to the Baptist's movement. Mark's gospel seems to imply this by saying that Jesus had no independent role until the Baptist was out of action. 'After John had been put in prison, Jesus went to Galilee and preached . . .' (1:14). John's gospel indicates this not only by its report that some of the apostles had been the Baptist's disciples (1:35-42), but also by its statement that Jesus spent some time baptizing near the Baptist (3:22, 23). The latter statement may have been too much for John's readers, since, in the gospel as we have it, it is contradicted by 4:2: 'Actually, Jesus himself did not baptize anyone; only his disciples did.'

A passage in Q is even stronger evidence that Jesus regarded the Baptist as 'much more than a prophet' and 'greater than any man who has ever lived' (Matthew 11:11). Matthew when reporting this adds that 'all the prophets and the Law of Moses, until the time of John, spoke about the Kingdom' – which implies that *John* was the climax of the whole Old Testament tradition. Luke says explicitly: 'The Law of Moses and the writings of the prophets were in effect up to the time of John the Baptist' (16:16). This is all the more surprising because we should expect both Matthew and Luke to say that the turning point was Jesus himself.

But there are also hints of tensions between the

Baptist and Jesus, and between their disciples. This Q passage begins with the Baptist's disciples asking Jesus: 'Are you the one John said was going to come, or should we expect someone else?' The reply of Jesus is a reference to the Book of Isaiah: 'The blind can see, the lame can walk, the lepers are made clean, the deaf hear, the dead are raised to life, and the Good News is preached to the poor.' But the puzzlement in the Baptist's circle is explained by a more homely reference to the popular opinion of Jesus: 'a glutton and wine-drinker, a friend of tax collectors and out-casts' (Matthew 11:19). It seems highly unlikely that the Christians should have invented such an unflattering remark about their holy saviour. The fact was that Jesus was no Puritan. Unlike the Baptist, his emphasis was not on condemnation but on fellowship; not on a warning but on an invitation to share a joy. His authority could not be understood without accepting John's right to baptism as coming from God (Mark 11: 27-33), but his mission was like a children's game of weddings while the Baptist's was like a game of funerals (Matthew 11:16-18).

The contrast between Jesus and the Baptist seems to show also the difference between Jesus and the Essenes. The probable site of Bathabara, the Baptist's head-quarters, lies only eight miles from the monastery at Qumran, and although the Baptist did not dress in the Essenes' white robes he may well have been influenced profoundly by their demand for purity. The Qumran monks took ritual baths every day, and John's essential message was that the whole of Israel needed to be washed clean of sin. The message of Jesus had many points in common with this holiness movement. But Jesus did not withdraw into the desert. He lived among the tax collectors and prostitutes. He taught the ignorant people where they were, in a language they could understand. And the image of the banquet was at the heart of his preaching.

3. Although he had worked as a carpenter, Jesus of Nazareth was widely welcomed as a teacher and a prophet.

In the Palestine where Jesus lived leadership in religion was strictly regulated, for everyone agreed that there were no prophets any more. The priests and Levites in the temple were hereditary. The 'teachers of the Law' or *rabbis* were carefully trained and solemnly ordained. No one ever said that Jesus was in either class. He was a layman. When the author of the Letter to the Hebrews wished to claim that Jesus was the perfect priest, he first had to face the facts that 'it is well known that he was born a member of the tribe of Judah', and 'no member of his tribe ever served as a priest at the altar' (7:13,14). When the author of the fourth gospel wished to present Jesus as delivering God's own teaching in the Court of the Gentiles in the temple (as any Jew was free to attempt), he first had to present the Jewish authorities as asking: 'How is it that this untrained man has such learning?' (7:15).

We have used the New English Bible's translation of that last question. In Today's English Version we read: 'How does this man know so much when he has never been to school?' But Jesus must have attended the school attached to the synagogue in Nazareth. From an unknown schoolmaster, as well as from his parents, he first acquired his knowledge and love of the Old Testament, while he 'grew, both in body and in wisdom' (Luke 2:52). The point of the question in John's gospel is surely that Jesus never attended a training course for rabbis. His school does not deserve to be completely forgotten.

Jesus is described by Mark (6:3) as a carpenter who belonged to a large family: he had four brothers and sisters as well. He is called by Matthew (13:55) 'the carpenter's son'; most jobs were then inherited. This need not mean that he was always poor. Carpenters were skilled craftsmen who made houses as well as agricultural implements and furniture. Since there is no mention of his father Joseph in the tradition after Matthew 2:23 and Luke 2:51, it is probable that Joseph died and that Jesus had to support the family, until he was 'about thirty'.

They lived in Nazareth, a little hillside town fifteen miles from the Lake of Galilee. The town had no fame or prestige. Matthew and Luke say that it did not even have the honour of being the birthplace of Jesus. We cannot and need not defend the complete historical accuracy of the stories surrounding the birth of Jesus in these two gospels. Almost all scholars nowadays treat them as being partly or entirely legends, although any reader with an eye for beauty or holiness will refrain from thinking they have nothing to say about the *meaning* of the coming of Jesus. But it is significant that Matthew and Luke wrote their gospels in the belief that Jesus of Nazareth had to be born in Bethlehem, the home town of King David. When Matthew wanted to produce some reference in the Old Testament to Nazareth, he quoted: 'He will be called a Nazarene' (2:23) – a quotation which no one has been able to trace in the Old Testament. In later controversy the Jewish rabbis called the Christians Nazarenes (*Nozri*), implying what Nathanael says in John's gospel: 'Can anything good come from Nazareth?' (1:46)

Galilee was (and is) a beautiful country. The historian Josephus, who once commanded the Jewish rebel army in Galilee, boasted of the land's fertility and the men's courage. There is some evidence that Galilee was also fertile in a courageous and enthusiastic kind of Judaism – as we should say 'charismatic' or spiritual religion with fewer rules and formalities. But Galilee was often despised by the inhabitants of Judea and Jerusalem. It was provincial; Peter was, we are told, recognized in the courtyard of the High Priest because of his rough accent, which no doubt Jesus shared. And Galilee had a mixed population, including many who were more Greek than Jewish. It is significant that the largest towns in Galilee, the Greek-speaking Sepphoris (only four miles to the north of Nazareth) and Tiberias, are not visited in the gospels. A devout Jew would avoid their pagan sights. This was 'Galilee of the Gentiles', as Matthew reminds his readers (4:15).

It is all the more remarkable that Jesus was so widely acknowledged as a teacher and prophet – and not only in 'charismatic' circles in Galilee. This tradition is preserved in the gospels although they might have been expected to divide the reactions between the hostility of the many and the worship of the few. Mark sums up the popularity of Jesus when he says that, in the last days in the Jerusalem temple, 'the large crowd heard Jesus gladly' (12:37). Jesus is frequently called 'Teacher'. In Mark's gospel people say: 'He is a prophet, like one of the prophets of long ago' (6:15; 8:28). In Luke's gospel the reaction produced by the report that Jesus has brought a dead man back to life is: 'A great prophet has appeared among us!' (7:16) And even at the end, the disciples walking to Emmaus call him simply 'Jesus of Nazareth . . . a prophet . . . considered by God and by all the people to

D

be mighty in words and deeds' (24:19).

One reason why Jesus was admired by many was that much of his teaching was the cream of the Old Testament and of contemporary Jewish religion. The gospels, although concerned to emphasize the novelty of Jesus, often show how orthodox he was in his loyalty to the Old Testament which he loved. For example, Mark (12:28-34) gives the story that he quoted from the two books, Deuteronomy and Leviticus, in answer to the question, 'Which commandment is the most important of all?' – and received the congratulations of the rabbi who asked him: 'Well done, Teacher!' Jesus was a teacher who simplified; in this, he must have seemed the successor of Hillel, the famous rabbi who flourished when Jesus was a boy. But he was more than a scholar. He was a prophet who made the ancient message vividly immediate.

The recorded teaching of Jesus includes a number of sayings which are similar to the recorded sayings of the rabbis. But the teaching of the rabbis includes much other material which seems to most modern readers far less alive and far less relevant.

Almost all modern Jewish scholars grant that Jesus had a genius for teaching. They agree, too, that he had a consistent style – pictorial rather than abstract, direct rather than allusive, sharp rather than full, exaggerated rather than qualified, sometimes terrifying but often witty, sometimes quoting the Old Testament but more often based on his own observation of nature and human life and his own direct knowledge of God. He did not waste words. What in an English translation looks like a certain amount of repetition was recognizable to all his first hearers as the 'parallelism' which was the strongest feature of Hebrew poetry (as the psalms show): something is said, and then either something in contrast or else something almost exactly the same. Indeed Jesus was a poet. In modern translations some passages of his teaching are printed as poetry. Many more could be. This style of Jesus was not exclusively his own; some of the rabbis sometimes spoke like this, and so did some of the early Christians (unless all the sayings which 'sound like sayings of Jesus' actually were his). But the two greatest thinkers of the first-century Church, Paul and John, had different styles, and almost all the Christian literature surviving from the second century is *very* different.

A prophet would be expected to speak with vividness and authority, as did the great prophets of Israel. Jesus did so. But he would also be expected to illustrate his teaching by symbolic actions, as when Jeremiah bought a field to show that prosperity would one day return to the country. Jesus did this, too.

4. Jesus performed many healings regarded as miraculous.

The gospels are full of the deeds of Jesus – healings welcomed as miracles, and understood as expulsions of the demons causing disease. This should not surprise us. There were some doctors, but not many; and they were not very effective. Mark 5:25-26, 'a woman who had suffered terribly . . . even though she had been treated by many doctors', is still more discouraging in the gospel of Doctor Luke: 'she had spent all she had on doctors, but no one had been able to cure her' (8:43). A prophet would be expected to heal. Why, the followers of the Pharisees did it! The Synoptic gospels make this point when reporting the Pharisees' objection that Jesus 'drives out demons only because their ruler Beelzebul gives him power to do so'. But in Q this passage ends with a claim which almost all scholars accept as a genuine saying of Jesus: 'It is God's Spirit who gives me the power to drive out demons, which proves that the Kingdom of God has already come upon you' (Matthew 12:22-28). The Greek of Luke's gospel (11:20) has 'by the finger of God I drive out demons', which may preserve the original best.

The accounts of these healings often mention the presence of faith and of sin (as in Mark 2:5). The explanation seems to be that many of these diseases were cured by strengthening the sufferer's will-power and sense of psychological liberation and calm. According to the translation of Mark 9:22-23 preferred in Today's English Version, Jesus when asked 'Help us, if you possibly can!' replied: 'Yes, if *you* can! Everything is possible for the person who has faith.' So many healings by the same method (they are often called 'faith-healing') have been attested in so many periods including our own that it is not reasonable to be completely sceptical. We may add that many of the diseases may have been partly mental in origin, or psychosomatic. In particular the word 'leprosy' was used of all kinds of skin diseases. In the absence of medical diagnosis some people believed to have died may in fact have been in a coma or 'sleep'.

This is not to say that as a matter of fact all these healings took place *exactly* as Christian preachers and gospel-writers were saying many miles away and thirty or fifty years later. That is highly improbable. Nor need we accept as historical facts all the non-healing miracles recounted in the gospels.

Some of these stories may be regarded as reliable, specially in view of many reports that Christian saints and non-Christian holy men have performed feats such as walking on water (Mark 6:45-52). Others of the stories may have grown in the telling. For example, we may ask: how many thousands were fed in the 'lonely place' – five thousand (Mark 6:30-44), or four thousand (Mark 8:1-10), or fewer? And we may ask: was new bread created, or were they fed by sharing their food when Jesus had taught and prayed? Was the real miracle the miracle of the new community? The strangest miracle in the gospels is often thought to be the cursing of the fig tree when Jesus 'found only leaves, because it was not the right time for figs' (Mark 11:12-14, 20-24). The explanation may be that the Church's tradition has misunderstood a parable which used the ripeness of the fig tree to teach about the ripeness of the time (Mark 13:28, 29 is an example).

The Synoptic gospels support the idea that the important deeds of Jesus were deeds of mercy to show the love of God. More than once they quote Jesus as explaining his work by quoting the compassionate acts of God prophesied in the Book of Isaiah (Matthew 11:5; Luke 4:18-19). And they tell in picture-language of how, after his baptism, Jesus was tempted by the Devil to perform miracles as a mere wonder-worker (Matthew 4:1-11; Luke 4:1-13). Mark's account of the feeding of the four thousand is prefaced by the simple words: 'I feel sorry for these people' (8:2). These words hold the key to the question: what matters today in the gospels' miracle-stories? For it may well be that behind them is what Jesus said was the most authentic reality in the world: God feeling sorry for his children and taking action to show he is King.

It is also worth noting that most of the accounts of miracles in the gospels are a great deal more restrained than those popular in pagan literature of the time. For example, there is no use made of a magic spell. Instead, Mark quotes and translates the simple commands of Jesus in Aramaic: *Talitha, koum* or 'Little girl (literally, little lamb)! Get up!' and *Ephphatha* or 'Open up!' (5:41; 7:34) In their version of the first of the healing miracles (they do not include the second), Matthew and Luke do not bother to report such homely words in the original language, so distant are they from the world where the magician depends on the formula of his incantation.

5. *Jesus broke religious laws and severely criticized religious leaders.*

Probing modern investigation of the evidence shows that it is highly probable that the gospels exaggerate the religious element in the trial of Jesus. The gospels were written at a time when the orthodox Jews certainly were accusing the Christians of blasphemy against God. Any orthodox Jew reading Paul's second letter to the Corinthians would have been horrified by the mention of a man before God in the letter's famous last sentence: 'The grace of the Lord Jesus Christ, the love of God . . .' But the claims made by Jesus in the Synoptic gospels do not amount to blasphemy as defined in the Jewish religious law. It was not blasphemy to claim to be 'Messiah' or 'Son of Man', and it is difficult to see why the High Priest 'tore his robes and said, "We don't need any more witnesses! You heard his wicked words" ' – as Mark claims (14:63). In any case the Jewish penalty for blasphemy was stoning, as Stephen was reminded (Acts 7:54-60). It is very probable that Jesus was arrested by the temple police as a trouble-maker and, after questioning, handed over to the Romans for crucifixion with the information that he was a rebel or potential rebel. There was only one trial – before Pilate.

But it is certain that Jesus clashed with the official religion of his day. The evidence surviving from the first century, both from the Christian and from the Jewish sides, has been shaped by the conflict of charge and counter-charge, but it speaks eloquently enough of the fact that Jesus was rejected by most of the rabbis despite his popularity as a prophet and healer. We have to account for this. In modern times many Jews have taken pride in the sublime ethics, the poetic genius, the courage, and the faith of Jesus the Jew – but clearly that was not the attitude of most of their first-century predecessors.

The explanation of this conflict is to be found in the evidence that Jesus broke the religious laws. The Law of God or *Torah* (which is really an untranslatable word, meaning much more than 'law') was reckoned to contain 248 positive commandments and 365 prohibitions. Jesus swept aside some of the most prominent of these.

One of the most sacred institutions of the Jewish religious system was the Sabbath. From Friday to Saturday evening, every Jew was commanded to rest from all work and to concentrate on the worship of God in the temple, synagogue or home. More than anything else this rule made the Jews distinctive in the Roman empire, and Julius Caesar won much credit from the Jews for allowing it to be observed. Jesus did not observe it strictly, although he was regular in his attendance at synagogue. Early in Mark's gospel comes the emphasis that Jesus made a point of performing on the Sabbath day cures which could easily have waited for the next day (1:21-28; 3:1-6). The same emphasis is found in the other gospels. Mark includes an incident when the breach of the Sabbath law had no great humanitarian purpose. Walking through some wheat fields, the disciples of Jesus 'began to pick the heads of wheat' and chew them. According to Mark Jesus defended them against critics. He recalled the example of King David and his soldiers who had eaten some sacred bread when hungry, and he concluded (in a phrase which could not be more relevant or explosive): 'The Sabbath was made for the good of man; man was not made for the Sabbath' (2:23-27).

Orthodox Jews of the first century (as of the twentieth) strictly obeyed many regulations about food – most of them probably imposed in the first place for hygienic purposes. Mark explains to his Gentile readers in Rome that 'the Pharisees, as well as the rest of the Jews . . . do not eat unless they wash their hands in the proper way . . . And they follow many other rules which they have received . . .' But Mark reports that some of the disciples of Jesus 'were eating their food with unclean hands' – and that again Jesus defended them, with the conclusion: 'There is nothing that goes into a person from the outside that can make him unclean' (7:1-23). Mark is interested in the incident because it seemed to show that 'Jesus declared that all foods are fit to be eaten' (7:19). Here Mark is going too far, because Paul's letters and the Acts of the Apostles show that there was an agonizing uncertainty among the first Christians about what foods could be eaten in the light of Jewish food laws or the pagan practice of giving a supper party to consume a joint left over from a sacrifice in a temple. But this report in Mark's gospel, repeated in Matthew's, does indicate a genuine controversy between Jesus and the teachers of the Law about cleanliness.

There is no evidence whether or not Jesus ever offered a sacrifice in the temple in Jerusalem. John may well be right in saying that every year as an adult Jesus made the journey to Jerusalem for the Passover feast; and Luke tells us that the practice began when Jesus was a boy with his parents (2:41). We know that many devout Jews kept the custom. Matthew is probably right to give this conversation: ' "Does your teacher pay the temple tax?" "Of course," Peter answered' (17:24, 25).

Mark also seems to be reporting the real situation when he quotes the instructions of Jesus to a 'leper' he has healed: 'Go straight to the priest and let him examine you; then offer the sacrifice that Moses ordered' (1:44). A similar order is given to ten lepers in Luke's gospel (17:14). A few aristocratic priests (the 'chief priests') lived in Jerusalem. From their families came the High Priests and the High Priest's Council, the *Sanhedrin*, before which Jesus appeared (Mark 14:53-65, etc.) – although this council also included leading laymen such as Gamaliel the Pharisee (Acts 5:34-40) and rich landowners such as Joseph of Arimathea (Mark 15:42-43). But most of the priests were on duty in the temple for only two weeks of the year. One of their few priestly duties while they were living ordinary lives back home was to testify that a 'leper' suffering from a skin disease was now 'clean' enough to be allowed to enter the temple and mix with neighbours. Apparently Jesus accepted such customs.

But that is not the end of the story. Mark reports that Jesus was accused of planning the destruction of the temple. We cannot be sure what, if anything, Jesus actually said. Not only does Mark tell us that those who accused Jesus 'could not make their stories agree' (14:59); the words reported in the gospel may well reflect the Christian belief that 'the temple Jesus spoke of was his body' (John 2:21). But according to

Mark the main accusation was that Jesus had said: 'I will tear down this temple which men made, and after three days I will build one that is not made by men' (14:58). Behind this there may lie a prophecy by Jesus that the temple would not last for ever. Rebuilt lavishly by Herod the Great, it was the centre of a proud and wealthy cult, subsidized by the temple tax paid by Jews all over the Roman empire. Under Annas (High Priest 16-18) and his son-in-law Caiaphas (High Priest 18-36), the aristocratic priests who ran this cult were all for peace and quiet, but there was a constant danger of the temple being identified with rebellion against Rome – as happened in 66-70. And other teaching by Jesus indicates his belief that the destruction of the temple would not be a complete calamity.

Like the great prophets of Israel, Jesus put righteousness before ritual, mercy before sacrifice. He advised: 'If you are about to offer your gift to God at the altar and there you remember that your brother has something against you, leave your gift there in front of the altar and go at once and make your peace with your brother' (Matthew 5:23-24). Christians such as Matthew recalled that vivid saying at a time when no Christian ever offered any sacrifice in any temple.

According to all four gospels, Jesus threw down a public challenge to the priests who had allowed the open-air Court of the Gentiles in the Jerusalem temple to become a sordid market for the sale of sacrificial animals – and for the exchange of coinage bearing the Roman Emperor's head for approved coins (which did not break the commandment against carving any representation of a man). Mark (11:15-19) gives the Old Testament quotation which Jesus used: 'My house will be called a house of prayer for all peoples'

– implying that the Gentiles had the right to a place for solemn worship. In addition to this misuse of the Court of the Gentiles, the very handsome profits made by the hereditary priests out of visitors to the temple had no doubt aroused the indignation of Jesus, who 'overturned the tables of the moneychangers and the stools of those who sold pigeons'.

The careful observance of so many regulations in the Law of God was regarded by orthodox Jews as a duty owed, and gladly paid, to the God who had shown his favour to Israel through the centuries. The temple was loved as a place where worship could be offered on behalf of Israel, and where sacrifices could be made as a sign of penitence and to restore fellowship with the holy God. Although the temple has never been rebuilt since its destruction by the Romans in 70 the Orthodox variety of Judaism still keeps the Law as it has inherited it, so that the spiritual strength and endurance of the tradition can still be experienced at first hand by modern man. Specially in modern dialogues between Christians and Jews – conversations almost always free of the hostility of the past – it is imperative for the followers of Jesus of Nazareth to be able to explain why their Master took the attitude which he did take.

It is possible to answer this question even if we exclude the gospels of Matthew and John as being too polemical to bear reliable witness. Mark implies much when he has Jesus defend the refusal of his disciples to fast, with the words: 'Do you expect the guests at a wedding party to go without food? Of course not!' (2:19) The message of Jesus is so joyful that this is no time for kill-joy prohibitions or inhibitions. Luke implies much when he gives the story of Jesus about the prayer of the Pharisee: 'I thank you,

God, that I am not greedy, dishonest, or immoral, like
everybody else . . . I fast two days every week, and I
give you one tenth of all my income' (18:11, 12). This
story does not mean that the Pharisee is greedy,
dishonest, or immoral. It does mean that he is so
preoccupied with his own struggle to be righteous
that he misses the joy of God's forgiveness.

No doubt some of the teachers of the Law were
hypocrites (a word which originally meant 'actors'), as
were some of the Pharisees (whose very name means
'the Separated'). Such men set themselves up as superior
to the ordinary 'people of the land' – and were naturally condemned by the people for acting their religion
hypocritically. And no doubt Jesus was a spokesman
for the layman's sense of priorities. Thus Mark
reports him as denouncing teachers who walk around in
their special robes and take reserved seats in the
synagogues – while robbing widows (12:38-40); and
Luke reports him as denouncing teachers who impose
strict laws on others without helping them to keep
them, and who build fine tombs for the old prophets
while being willing to condemn those who now carry
on the old prophets' work (11:45-52). Luke adds that
Jesus also denounced Pharisees who sanctimoniously
gave to God a tenth even of seasoning herbs – but
neglected to give love to God or to seek justice for
men. Such men were like graves which had not been
white-washed in order to warn passers-by of the
danger of pollution by touching them (Luke 11:44).
They were men who with elaborate care would strain a
fly out of a drink – and swallow a camel without
noticing (Matthew 23:24).

It is, however, impossible to believe that Jesus, who is
normally shown as a just and merciful judge, condemned *all* the teachers of the Law and *all* the Pharisees

for being hypocrites *all* the time. Such an attitude would have severed all relations with them, yet the tradition says that teachers of the Law were frequently in conversation with Jesus and some Pharisees were on friendly terms with him – such as the Pharisee at whose table Jesus is said to have delivered that denunciation (Luke 11:37), or Simon the Pharisee who 'invited Jesus to have dinner with him' (7:36). In modern times Jewish and Christian scholars have joined in an attempt to do justice to these first-century teachers and Pharisees.

We can see that they differed not only from the 'people of the land' but also from most of the priests. The Jewish priests all inherited the priesthood from their fathers. We can safely assume that most of them thought that being a priest meant discharging their ceremonial duties in the temple, giving the blessing in the local synagogue, and observing the regulations of purity. Judaism needed other religious leadership, and this was provided by the teachers of the Law and the Pharisees. Some conscientious priests became teachers, and some became Pharisees, but many laymen joined these orders while continuing to earn their livings as farmers, tradesmen, and so forth. The teachers or rabbis wore a special robe, but were distinguished also by having pursued for several years a course of study (in the sacred language, Hebrew, rather than in the popular language, Aramaic). The Pharisees insisted on a special purity in their food and had meals in common as religious communities; Josephus, who had belonged to this order himself, tells us that they numbered about six thousand. Most teachers were not Pharisees, and most Pharisees were not teachers, but one who had been both assured the Christians in Philippi that he had certainly not been a hypocrite. 'So

far as keeping the Jewish law is concerned,' Paul wrote,
'I was a Pharisee' (3:5).

It is inaccurate to group all these men together
for the same praise as Israel's élite; but it is even
more inaccurate to group them together in total condemnation. It says much for them that even Matthew
in his very severe account shows that they were given the
best seats and were 'greeted with respect in the market
places' (23:6, 7). It says even more about their standing
in Jewish public opinion that they were able to reconstruct the Jewish religion when the temple was rubble.
The chief theme of the criticism of the teachers of
the Law and the Pharisees by Jesus must, it seems, have
been that expressed by Luke in the last third of the
parable of the lost son (15:25-32). There the older son
is proud of his obedient service of his father, and his
father does not contradict his claims. But this obedient
son has missed what is in his father's heart by re-
fusing to join the happy feast of forgiveness. And the
reason why he refuses is pride.

The gospels' reports of the attitude of Jesus to the
religious leaders has been influenced by the bitterness of
the break between church and synagogue. But there is
no need to doubt that Jesus voiced his criticisms of the
pride of the religious leaders of his own people with
seriousness and urgency. His whole message led up to
the announcement of a crisis. It would be to him
a terrible tragedy that most of these religious leaders
should reject his message and person, and actually
encourage the pride which was to lead to the suicidal rebellion against Rome. A passage in Q catches this
attitude to the holy city and to what it represents:
'Jerusalem, Jerusalem! You kill the prophets and stone
the messengers God has sent you! How many times have
I wanted to put my arms round all your people, just as

a hen gathers her chicks under her wings, but you
would not let me!' (Matthew 23:37)

*6. Jesus became the friend of the disreputable, teaching
the unconditional love of God and man.*

One of the strongest themes in the tradition about
Jesus is announced by Mark (2:16, 17). 'Some teachers
of the Law, who were Pharisees, saw that Jesus was
eating with these outcasts and tax collectors; so they
asked his disciples, "Why does he eat with such people?"
Jesus heard them and answered, "People who are well
do not need a doctor, but only those who are sick. I
have not come to call the respectable people, but the
outcasts." ' The true tradition breaks through the pre-
judice which Matthew still reflects. For Matthew says
that a man who does not listen to the Church should
be treated 'as though he were a foreigner or a tax collector' (18:17) – but he is truer to the mind of Jesus
when he gives the saying: 'the tax collectors and the
prostitutes are going into the Kingdom of God ahead of
you' (21:31). The fact is clear that Jesus took many
meals with prostitutes and with the tax collectors who
were hated because they perpetrated many cruel rackets
in the service of the foreign oppressor. It is an astonishing fact to record about a man who taught a lofty
religion and morality.

The explanation is given when we are told what Jesus
taught about God and man. He taught that God for-
gave sins gladly – and to prove it, he himself would
say without hesitation: 'My son, your sins are forgiven'
(as in Mark 2:5). The rabbis and Pharisees no doubt
considered that this made the forgiveness of God
cheap. According to the orthodox Jewish piety,
God's mercy had to be entreated with many prayers
and tears; it had to be sought by many sacrifices in the

temple, if at all possible; it had to be deserved by a life of obedient goodness. But according to Jesus God was like a father who actually *ran* to greet a son who was 'still a long way from home' – and who instantly gave back all a son's privileges (Luke 15: 20-23).

The message of Jesus was about receiving the forgiveness of the loving God – and showing that one has received it by an unconditional love for God and man. The model prayer given by Jesus to his disciples includes the striking petition: 'Forgive us our sins, *as* we forgive everyone who does us wrong' (Luke 11:4). Today's English Version misses the point with its '*because* we forgive . . .' People are entitled to ask for God's forgiveness *to the precise extent* that they are willing to forgive others. People who have been really forgiven will really love. In the parable given by Matthew the man who demands the immediate repayment of 'a few pounds' although he has just had his own debts of 'millions of pounds' wiped out is not forgiven (18:21-35). And in Luke's gospel Simon the Pharisee is told at dinner: 'Do you see this woman? . . . The great love she has shown proves that her many sins have been forgiven' (7:44, 47).

The prostitutes, the tax collectors, and the 'people of the land' from whom the Pharisees pointedly separated themselves – these disreputable people were an attentive audience for such a message. It was to 'many tax collectors and outcasts' that Jesus first told the story of the foolish young man who still trusted his father solely because he was his father, and who was welcomed back solely because he was a son (Luke 5: 11-24).

7. Jesus announced that the Kingdom of God was near by telling parables.

The actions of Jesus spoke louder than words. When he healed someone, that action shouted aloud that God was King. When he sat next to someone, that said very effectively that God was Friend. But he also used words as weapons.

He was a master of the short story with a religious point. Some parables are to be found elsewhere in the New Testament and in other ancient Christian literature, but in comparison with those in the Synoptic gospels they are clumsy – for example, Paul's parable of the olive tree in his letter to the Romans (11:16-18). Parables are also to be found in the teaching of the rabbis and in the Old Testament, but no teacher of Israel known to us used parables half as much, or half as well, as Jesus. The Synoptic gospels show that this was his favourite method of teaching the public. Even Mark shows this, although (in accordance with his belief that Jesus kept his identity a secret although this was the core of his message) he has to claim that the parables were told in order that people should *not* see and understand (4:10-12)! Matthew and Luke repeat this odd claim from Mark, but Luke clearly believes that the parables he gives make their point with very little explanation – and Matthew adds another of his Old Testament quotations: 'I will tell them things unknown since the creation of the world' (13:35).

In his book *Rediscovering the Teaching of Jesus* (p. 83), Dr Norman Perrin has summed up the studies of other modern scholars to show that the major parables of Jesus originally had various aims. Here we use the titles added in Today's English Version.

Two parables were 'concerned to emphasize the joyousness with which the activity of God may be experienced' – the Hidden Treasure and the Pearl, given only by Matthew (13:44-46). Others were 'concerned to express the challenge of the major aspect of this divine activity, the forgiveness of sins' – the Lost Sheep, the Lost Coin, the Lost Son (Luke 15).

Some parables were 'concerned with the necessity for men to decide *now*' – the Great Feast which is in Q (the better version is in Luke 14:15-24) and the Shrewd Manager (Luke 16:1-8). Others were 'concerned to warn against the danger of preconceived ideas blinding one to the reality of the challenge'. Three examples are given by Matthew: the Workers in the Vineyard (20:1-16), the Two Sons (21:28-32), the Children in the Market Place (11:16-19). One is given by Luke: the Pharisee and the Tax Collector (18:9-14). Still other parables were 'concerned to depict the various aspects and true nature of the necessary response to the challenge'. Examples are the Good Samaritan (Luke 10:25-37), the Unforgiving Servant (Matthew 18:23-35), and the two parables about the cost of being a disciple: the Tower-builder and the King Going to War (Luke 14:28-33).

Finally, two parables given by Luke were 'concerned to stress the confidence in God which the experience of his activity should bring' (the friend asked for bread at night, 11:5-8, and the judge asked for justice by the widow, 18:1-8) – while others are specially 'concerned to stress the confidence in God's future which the experience of his activity in the present should bring'. Three examples of this last group are given by Matthew: the Weeds (13:24-30), the Yeast (13:33), and the Net (13:47-50). Three come in Mark's gospel: the Sower (4:1-9), the Growing Seed (4:26-29), and the Mustard Seed (4:30-32).

Dr Perrin's classification is illuminating. However,

other scholars divide the parables in other ways, and it is certainly curious that Dr Perrin has not included in this list some parables which are listed at the back of the epoch-making *Parables of Jesus* by Joachim Jeremias. These include the Return of the Evil Spirit which is in Q (Matthew 12:43-45) and the Rich Man and Lazarus (Luke 16:19-31) – memorable warnings. But special attention ought to be given to the Tenants in the Vineyard, included by Mark (12:1-12) and used also by Matthew and Luke; the Man Who Goes Away from Home (Mark 13:32-37); the Thief Breaking In (Matthew 24:43-44, also in Luke); the Faithful or the Unfaithful Servant (Matthew 24:45-51, also in Luke); the Ten Girls, the Three Servants, and the Final Judgement (all in Matthew 25); the Rich Fool, the Watchful Servants, the Unfruitful Fig Tree, and the Closed Door (all in Luke 12:13-21; 12:35-40; 13:6-9; 13:22-30). For all these twelve parables emphasize the urgency of the crisis brought about by God's activity, and there is no good reason to believe that they are less genuine than the parables of Jesus which do appear in Dr Perrin's list.

Many of the parables of Jesus are reported in the gospels with explanations (for example, Mark 4:13-20) or with shorter moralizing comments (for example, Matthew 20:16 or Luke 16:9-13). There is no space here to give the reasons for believing that most of these explanations or comments were not added by Jesus; the arguments were presented by Dr Jeremias. It will be enough to note that most scholars now regard these passages as the editorial work of the Christian Church. In most cases the explanation or comment seems to be aimed at making the parable clearly relevant to the problems of the Church when the gospels were being written, specially the problem of the delay in the coming of the End. Either an explanation by a preacher (or by the gospel-writer himself) would be inserted after the parable, or a saying of Jesus would be added because it was thought to be relevant.

It is almost certain that originally each of the parables was told with one main point in mind; the elaborate explanations of what each detail meant all came later. The parable was told so that this one point would sink into the memories of the first hearers, although many of them did not immediately understand or respond. They would go away relishing the story and thinking quietly about its significance. And it is almost certain that originally the parables were told in order to encourage or warn about the coming of the Kingdom of God. The message of Jesus through them was that God's activity was about to reach a climax, proving his reality and establishing his rule.

Mark sums up the message of Jesus: 'The right time has come and the Kingdom of God is near! Turn away from your sins and believe the Good News!' (1:15) Matthew and Luke confirm this. Mark also makes it plain what 'near' means. 'Remember this! There are some here who will not die until they have seen the Kingdom of God come with power' (9:1). Matthew (16:28) and Luke (9:27) confirm this, too, although they slightly change this saying of Jesus in order to make it fit more easily into their own editorial tendencies. 'There are some here who will not die until they have seen the Son of Man come as King.' 'There are some here, I tell you, who will not die until they have seen the Kingdom of God.'

What, then, was the 'secret of the Kingdom of God' which Jesus told (Mark 4:11)? Obviously the idea had many aspects. If that had not been the case, Jesus would not have had to tell so many stories in order to illustrate it. But almost all scholars agree that Jesus did *not* expect the coming Kingdom to be confined to a change in the attitudes of individuals.

The phrases constantly quoted by those who advocate an exclusively psychological interpretation of the idea of the Kingdom are 'the Kingdom of God does not come in such a way as to be seen' and 'the Kingdom of God is within you' – as Today's English Version translates Luke 17:20-21. Admittedly Luke's Greek, which is ambiguous, can have this meaning. But the translation preferred in the New English Bible is better: 'The Pharisees asked him, "When will the Kingdom of God come?" He said, "You cannot tell by observation when the Kingdom of God comes. There will be no saying, 'Look, here it is!' or 'there it is!'; for in fact the Kingdom of God is among you." ' Other possible translations of that last phrase, mentioned in the New English Bible footnotes, are: 'in fact the Kingdom of God is within your grasp' or 'suddenly the Kingdom of God will be among you.'

The last translation seems the most in keeping with what Luke's gospel goes on to teach: 'Don't go out looking for' the Kingdom in response to those who point out the signs, saying 'Look, over there!' or 'Look, over here!' – for the day of the Son of Man when it comes will be like lightning which 'flashes across the sky and lights it up from one side to the other'. The translation that the Kingdom of God is or will be *among* you' also connects more closely with the rest of the teaching of Jesus, where everywhere the Kingdom of God appears as God's rule over the whole earth, not as a change *within* individuals. In addition we should notice that the phrase about the Kingdom being 'among you' was, according to Luke, spoken to 'some Pharisees' – who in this gospel do not appear as men already possessing the Kingdom of God *within* their hearts.

The neatest definition of the idea of the Kingdom of God is, we may conclude, given in Matthew's version of the Lord's Prayer:

'may your Kingdom come;
may your will be done on earth as it is in heaven'
(6:10).

The report in Mark's gospel about the instructions to the twelve apostles about their first mission certainly suggests urgency (6:6-13). This impression is heightened by the first part of the instructions in Matthew's gospel (10:5-15, 23). But we cannot recover much of the psychology of Jesus. In this instance, Matthew also contemplates a mission to rulers, kings, and the Gentiles (10:16-22, based on Mark 13:9-13). What we can be reasonably sure of is that Jesus looked forward at his last supper to drinking 'the new wine in the Kingdom of God' (Mark 14:25) and to eating the Passover meal when 'it is given its full meaning in the Kingdom of God' (Luke 22:16). The early Christians waited for Jesus to come back from heaven while some of them were alive, as Paul wrote in his first letter to the Thessalonians (1:10; 4:15). It seems highly unlikely that they would have held this hope unless they had thought that the historical Jesus had so hoped.

Since the original message of Jesus was that God's all-embracing Kingdom was near, its impact was like an electric shock. The proclamation was made in a series of short stories of dazzling brilliance. And the promise or the challenge was that those who first heard these stories *would soon see for themselves*. This, and nothing less than this, accounts for the stir made by the teaching of Jesus. For the first hearers of Jesus were being described as the last generation, face to face with the last destiny.

8. Exercising his personal authority, Jesus summoned and sent out messengers to Israel; and the message he gave them was potentially for all mankind.

All the evidence agrees that Jesus spoke and acted with authority, and that the authority which he claimed was more than that expected in a teacher or prophet. In Q there was a saying: 'My Father has given me all things. No one knows the Son except the Father, and no one knows the Father except the Son, and those to whom the Son wants to reveal him' (Matthew 11:27). Scholars disagree about the authenticity of this saying. It sounds suspiciously like John's gospel. But it has been suggested that only the capital letters in a modern translation represent the Church's use of the titles 'the Father' and 'the Son'. (The earliest Greek manuscripts we have were entirely written in capital letters.) The meaning may well be that Jesus understands God as a son understands his father. On that basis many scholars accept the saying as genuine – as a reflection of the unique relationship which the historical Jesus claimed with God, and as an expression of his claim to a unique authority.

One way in which Jesus showed his authority was by choosing his followers and demanding that they should give up literally everything – wives, children, jobs, possessions, opinions – in order to be with him. He did not urge this on everyone. According to Mark one man whom he had cured offered to follow him and was told to go home (5:18, 19). But with those he wanted, he was ruthless. According to Luke, one man was willing to follow him if he could first go back home

and bury his father. The reply of Jesus was: 'Let
the dead bury their own dead. You go and preach the
Kingdom of God' (9:59, 60).

Later, hostile rabbis were to say that Jesus had
five special assistants; Josephus was to give the figure
as 150. The Synoptic gospels give twelve (Mark
3:13-19, with slightly different accounts in Matthew
and Luke), and Luke adds a further seventy-two (10:
1-23). These were given authority to cure diseases and
spread the message. Their education had been in the
synagogue schools of their boyhoods and in the
travelling school conducted by Jesus himself; but the
prayer of Jesus given in Q expresses (almost as well
as the sublime chapters of John) his love of, and
union with, these humble men. 'Father, Lord of heaven
and earth! I thank you because you have shown to the
unlearned what you have hidden from the wise and
learned. Yes, Father, this was done by your own
choice and pleasure' (Matthew 11:25, 26).

It lies beyond doubt that Jesus associated others
intimately with his work. It is also clear that Jesus
expected others to share his glory. Not only do all the
gospels say so repeatedly. It is inconceivable that Jesus
thought of a reward for himself alone, since the
whole emphasis of the Old Testament and of the Jewish
religion, from first to last, was on the people of God
and its future. All the mysterious figures symbolising
the Jewish experience and hope – Messiah, Servant, Son
of Man – were related to the people of God. The Bible
knows no such thing as a solitary Christ. Luke's gospel
is based on that fact (at least) when it quotes the
promise of Jesus to his disciples at their last supper:
'You will eat and drink at my table in my Kingdom,
and you will sit on thrones to judge the twelve tribes of
Israel' (22:30).

One of the strongest features of the Synoptic gospels, historically speaking, is their admission that the historical Jesus was a thorough Jew, who thought as a Jew and who worked only among fellow-members of the twelve tribes. It must have been very tempting for Mark, who wrote in Rome, and for Luke, who wrote for the Roman empire, to pretend that Jesus was at heart a Gentile, transcending all the limitations of his surroundings. Matthew, too, writing for Jews when disaster had overtaken the Jewish nation, must have been tempted to present a Jesus who from the first had had his eyes set on 'all peoples everywhere' (28:19). The gospel-writers do not make that pretence. Instead, they all state clearly that the mission of Jesus and his apostles before his death was 'not to any Gentile territory' but 'only to the lost sheep of the people of Israel' (Matthew 10:5, 6; 15:24).

However, if God's offer was as the historical Jesus said it was, it could not be confined for ever to Jews. The restriction of the mission of Jesus and his apostles to Israel resulted from the limitations of time and energy; it was not a matter of profound and permament principle. We have already noted the hints in Luke's gospel of the coming spread of 'the Good News' from Jerusalem to Rome. But the same point is made in Mark's gospel, copied by Matthew: having at first refused to help a woman because she is a foreigner, Jesus agrees in answer to her wit and faith (7:24-30). The point is also made in the Q story of the healing of the Roman officer's servant (Matthew 8:5-13).

Why, then, was there such hesitation in the early Church about the wisdom of preaching to Gentiles, and why was there such controversy about the terms on which they might be baptized into the Church? The details of the delays and difficulties of the Gentile mission have not been preserved with a complete accuracy, but the impression left by Paul's letters and the Acts of the Apostles is clear and convincing. In the fierce debate about the admission of Gentiles who have not first become Jews, no one ever appeals to the historical Jesus as having settled the problem. The most likely explanation is that what little Jesus said about any future appeal to the Gentiles was clothed in the Old Testament's imagery of the Gentiles *going to Jerusalem* in repentance and faith when they saw the glory in Israel at the End. As the Q passage puts it: 'Many will come from the east and the west and sit down . . .' (Matthew 8:11). A vast mission to the Gentiles in Gentile territory was not in mind. On the other hand, the use of this imagery did not rule out any possibility of such a mission. In the time of Jesus orthodox Jews, inspired by the Old Testament, conducted extensive missionary activities among Gentiles. As Matthew has it: 'You sail the seas and cross whole countries to win one convert' (23:15).

9. *Jesus disclaimed knowledge of the exact date of the End, and foretold great suffering for himself, his followers, and his people.*

Deeply embedded in the early Christian tradition is the denial of knowledge exactly when the End would come. All the enthusiasm about the near End always included this reserve. Mark, when he has just used the prophecy that 'all these things will happen before the people now living have all died' (13:30), adds the saying: 'No one knows, however, when that day or hour will come – neither the angels in heaven, nor the Son; only the Father knows' (13:32). The saying is repeated by Matthew (24:36). It deserves to be weighed together with the Q saying that the Son of Man will come like a thief in the night, 'at an hour when you are not expecting him' (Matthew 24:43, 44) – a comparison also made by Paul in his first letter to the Thessalonians (5:2).

If the first Christians had been able to quote from Jesus an exact prediction enabling them to know when to expect the End, they would no doubt have done so – because it was an age keenly interested in such prophecies, and the material collected in all three Synoptic gospels (specially Mark 13, Matthew 24, and Luke 12 and 21) shows how fascinated the Christians were by signs of the coming End. It is almost certain that such collections of signs were revised to take account of events such as the attempt of the Emperor Caligula to install a statue of himself in the Jerusalem temple in 40 (this seems to have been the 'Awful Horror' which the reader of Mark 13:14 is told to understand) or the fall of Jerusalem thirty years later. However the main thrust of the Christian teaching was that when the End really came its signs would be clear enough. They would be, as Luke reports, like the flash of lightning in a thunderstorm (17:24), or like the vultures round a dead body (17:37). And with that, the Christians had to try to be content.

This evidence of a caution and a reverence, reserving knowledge of the date of the End to God alone, is what we should expect of devout Jews. The great prophets of the Old Testament often claimed to be proclaiming the intentions of God, but they were not fortune-tellers whose reputations entirely depended upon exact predictions of the future. Above all the heirs of the piety of the Old Testament would have abhorred as blasphemous any suggestion that they should force God's hand into acting in the way they expected. Always God was left with his sovereignty. Albert Schweitzer's reconstruction of the historical Jesus (see page 12) is for this reason psychologically impossible.

One theme is clear in many reports of what Jesus expected. He foretold *suffering* for himself, his followers, and his people, before the End. No doubt the reports which we have in the gospels have been phrased in the knowledge of what took place, but we have no good reason to reject them entirely. It needed only common sense, not the intuitive genius of a prophet, to see that a man liable to be called 'King of the Jews' was liable to be crucified in first-century Palestine, and that even if they escaped with their lives his followers were liable to face unpopularity, despair, and actual punishment after his execution. It also needed only common sense to see that the pride of the Jews was such that rebellion against Rome was inevitable, and that rebellion would bring catastrophe. And such expectations fitted in well with the general Jewish belief of the time that the coming glories of the messianic age would be preceded by a time of sufferings, the 'birthpangs of the Messiah'.

The fact that Jesus expected suffering is confirmed by the model prayer which he taught. 'Do not bring us to hard testing' refers to the trials in the future, before the End (Luke 11:4). These trials were expected to be so severe that faith, courage, and obedience might falter.

A man such as Jesus is known to have been cannot have voiced such expectations without showing an anguished disappointment and a sensitivity to the spiritual and physical tragedies involved for the people and the places he loved. Three reports in the gospels are poignantly in keeping with his character. As Luke reports, Jesus told Peter on that last night: 'I have prayed for you, Simon, that your faith will not fail' (22:32) – and next morning he said to the women of Jerusalem: 'Don't cry for me, but for yourselves and your children' (23:28). And, according to a report in Q, he lamented over three obscure Galilean towns: 'How terrible it will be for you, Chorazin! How terrible for you too, Bethsaida! . . . And as for you, Capernaum! You wanted to lift yourself up to heaven? You will be thrown down to hell!' (Matthew 11:20-24)

10. Jesus believed that his death lay within the purpose of God, and after it his followers became convinced that on this as on other matters he was right.

The fact that Jesus was betrayed by one of his twelve chosen apostles is often repeated in the gospels, and there is no good reason to doubt it. The story was no advertisement either for the apostles or for their training. Exactly what secret Judas Iscariot betrayed, and precisely why he did it, we cannot tell. The gospels suggest that he betrayed the secret of when Jesus could be arrested quietly, and did it for money, yet was stricken with remorse and hanged himself. Many have looked for a deeper explanation. Did Judas betray the secret that Jesus would now admit to claiming the Messiahship? If he was a patriotic Zealot, did he attempt to force his Master's hand into launching a rebellion in order to escape death? Did his game go terribly wrong? All these are speculations. All we can know is that, if Judas ended up a simple suicide, Jesus did not.

The Synoptic gospels never explain at any length why Jesus laid down his life. Mark, as we have seen, mentions that the death of Jesus was the price paid to liberate many people and the sealing of a new agreement between God and man (10:45; 14:24). Matthew and Luke do little more than to repeat these clues. The three gospels do, however, provide another clue in the shape of the story of the 'transfiguration' of Jesus (Mark 9:2-13, etc.). It is a story which is mysterious and may have been embroidered in the telling. But essentially it rings true, for it is a record of a mystical experience in which Jesus felt that he was talking with Moses, with Elijah, and ultimately with God himself about his own coming death. This took place 'up a high mountain', presumably Mount Hermon, and Jesus was accompanied by Peter, John, and James, who were somehow affected by the intense experience of their Master. At the end 'only Jesus was with them' – a Jesus strengthened in the faith that his death was in accordance with the teaching of the Old Testament and the will of God.

The story of the last supper of Jesus with his disciples is another such clue. It seems certain that Jesus did then link his death with the coming of the Kingdom of God. The saying in Mark's gospel must have puzzled those who read it in the first century, as it has puzzled Christians since: 'I tell you, I will never again drink this wine until the day I drink the new wine in the Kingdom of God' (14:25). That is an argument for the substantial authenticity of the saying. Above all, we have the saying over the bread, repeated countless times by Christians in the first century as in every later age: 'Take it, this is my body' (14:22). Such a saying is so obviously liable to lead to a rumour of cannibalism (as it certainly did) that it is hard to believe that extremely devout Christians with a Jewish training, such as Paul or Mark, could have invented it. As the loaf of bread was broken and given, so the life of Jesus was being broken and given;

and Jesus said so.

The third highly relevant story is of the distress of Jesus before his death. It comes in the Letter to the Hebrews: 'In his life on earth Jesus made his prayers and requests with loud cries and tears to God, who could save him from death' (5:7). Mark gives us a picture of Jesus praying in 'distress and anguish' during the night before he was tortured to death. 'Father! My Father! All things are possible for you. Take this cup away from me. But not what I want, but what you want' (14:32-36). Virtually the same picture of the Lord Jesus in weakness is given by Matthew and Luke, and it is not a picture the early Christians would have cared to invent.

All the evidence in the Synoptic gospels points to a man who was careful not to fall into the hands of his enemies – until he deliberately and publicly went to Jerusalem at the time of the Passover feast. He could easily have remained in comparative safety, outside the city where his enemies and the Roman soldiers could be expected to gather at that time. If he had merely wished to worship in the temple, he could have done so without allowing a provocative demonstration and without issuing his own public challenges in his teaching. He risked death. He almost courted it. A man so devout and so shrewd would never have done so except after self-searching prayer. It therefore seems certain that Jesus believed in the depths of his being that it was his Father's will that he should accept the cross.

So he was scourged and hung up to die. The best attested cry from the cross is the one which causes the most pain in any Christian who records it: 'My God, my God, why did you abandon me?' (Mark 15:34, also in Matthew). That is the terrible voice of history, the cry of human anguish. It is a quotation from Psalm

22, where the despair moves into faith. Whether or not
Jesus before he died experienced and voiced a calm
faith – as Matthew, Luke, and John report – we do know
that Mark and Matthew, who preserved this cry of
despair, believed passionately that the despair was not
ultimate, for they believed that the crucified had been
crowned as the Messiah and as the Son of God. They
were already on the road which led Luke and John in
their gospels to present this horrible death, accepted in
faith and in love for others, as itself part of the glory
of the divine love. So these gospels of Luke and John
give us the deeply moving and even joy-making features
of the full Christian tradition about the Passion of Jesus.
They ploclaim the death as it releases forgiveness, gives
the assurance of Paradise, perfectly sums up a life of
trust in the Father, binds all Christians together in
a new family, and finishes the revelation of the light that
shines on all men.

Some modern writers, seeking to explain the reports
that Jesus was seen alive after his crucifixion, have
speculated that he was not dead when taken down from
the cross. They imagine him reviving, and being
nursed back into some sort of existence in hiding. But
it is extremely unlikely that Roman soldiers would
have left an execution uncompleted, even if they had
had any motive to do so. Such a lapse from duty would
certainly have meant death to them, when discovered.

Other modern writers have suggested that the
corpse was taken to the common criminals' grave in
the Valley of Hinnom (that nauseating rubbish dump
which provided the imagery of hell), not to a private
tomb provided by Joseph of Arimathea as reported in
the gospels. On historical grounds we cannot be so sure
where Jesus was buried as we can be sure *that* he
was buried. On the other hand, if the story of the

private burial is a Christian invention it is strange that
the name of Joseph of Arimathea is given by all the
gospels with such confidence. It therefore seems
reasonable to accept the tradition that Jesus was
buried in a private tomb whose ownership was known
to some of his despairing ex-followers. It has been
suggested that his followers were not clear exactly
where the tomb was, and that the women who later went
to embalm the body went to the wrong tomb, which
was empty. Here again we cannot tread on safely
historical ground, because the evidence is so fragmen-
tary. But it is worth noting that when Matthew wrote
the official Jewish story it was that the followers of
Jesus went to the *right* tomb – and stole his body
(28:11-15). Psychologically, this is an unlikely tale. If
the body was removed from the tomb, it is more likely
that the Romans did the removing. But if we confine
our investigation to a strict use of the modern historian's methods, we shall find that the 'ifs' are
endless.

The mental agony of Jesus, expressed in the prayer in
Gethsemane and in the cry that God had abandoned
him, was so great that many modern students of the
gospels find it impossible to accept completely their
statement that Jesus was sure that he would be raised
from death after a short interval. Equally, the bewilderment and despair of the disciples – to be expected after
the horror of the crucifixion, and clearly reflected in the
gospels – persuade many modern students that the resurrection of Jesus on the third day was not expected
and therefore had not been predicted as precisely as the
gospels say. The phrasing of the predictions which we
find in the gospels – including 'after three days he
will rise to life' at Mark 8:31 – may well have been
coloured by the Church's reflection on the prophecy in

E

the Book of Hosea: 'after two days he will heal us, on
the third day we shall rise up' (6:2). What *is* psychologically possible, and in keeping with all the evidence we have, can be put quite simply. Jesus
trusted that he would be vindicated by God at the
End; but since he disclaimed knowledge of when
the End would come, he died on the Friday without
knowing that his victory would be declared on the
Sunday.

One of the features of the End, as expected by many,
was the physical resurrection of the dead. We find
this belief stated in the Book of Daniel, written just
over a century and a half before the birth of Jesus.
At that time many Jews had been put to death because
they had refused to renounce the peculiarities of their
religion, at a time when great pressure had been
applied by the political rulers to fit Judaism into the
culture of the Greek world. The cause of Jewish
separation had then triumphed temporarily through the
rebellion led by the Maccabees, but the conviction had
grown among many Jews that the martyrs would be
rewarded and their persecutors punished – and the
only way in which such rewards and punishments would
be effective had been thought to be the resurrection of
their dead bodies by the divine Judge.

In the time of Jesus the Pharisees held this belief
strongly, and in the Acts of the Apostles Paul defends
himself on this ground: 'My brothers! I am a Pharisee,
the son of Pharisees. I am on trial here because I hope
that the dead will rise to life!' (23:6) But the Pharisees
were themselves the products of the religious crisis in
the days of the Maccabees, and the belief was rejected by more conservative Jews who regarded as
authoritative only the first five books in our Old
Testament. As Luke explained to his Gentile readers in

Acts: 'the Sadducees say that people will not rise from death, and that there are no angels or spirits; but the Pharisees believe in all three' (23:8). The Sadducees were a small religious party composed largely of the priests of the Jerusalem temple, but they appear in the gospels asking Jesus a cynical question about the time 'when all the dead rise to life on the day of resurrection'. According to this report, Jesus told them that they were 'completely wrong', for the dead *do* rise to life (Mark 12:18-27). There is no good reason to doubt that this was one of a large number of beliefs which he held in common with the Pharisees.

In the next chapter we shall consider what happened after the burial of Jesus. But what happened then was not so public as the work and teaching of Jesus of Nazareth, the subject of this chapter; nor can it be known so certainly. By doing what he did, and by saying what he said, Jesus set up the public sign which he intended. If people rejected that sign, it was highly unlikely that they would be persuaded by any reported miracle. As Luke's gospel puts it, 'if they will not listen to Moses and the prophets, they will not be convinced even if someone were to rise from death' (16:31).

Mark reports Jesus as groaning and saying: 'Why do the people of this generation ask for a miracle? No, I tell you! No such proof will be given this people!' (8:12) Matthew, when reporting this saying, adds: 'You ask me for a miracle? No! The only miracle you will be given is the miracle of Jonah' (16:4). In Q this miracle is explained: 'In the same way that Jonah spent three days and nights in the belly of the big fish, so will the Son of Man spend three days and nights in the depths of the earth' (Matthew 12:40). The trouble about this explanation is that, as we have seen, Jesus is unlikely to have predicted a stay in his tomb of precisely three days and nights. (Incidentally, according to the Easter stories, Jesus did not spend more than two nights in the tomb!) Many scholars therefore regard this explanation as the work of the Church, which compared the resurrection of Jesus with Jonah's escape from the whale. It seems probable that originally Jesus referred to *his preaching* as the only 'miracle' he was offering to the public. Another saying in Q would then be an apt comment: 'On the Judgement Day the people of Nineveh will stand up and accuse you, because they turned from their sins when they heard Jonah preach; and there is something here, I tell you, greater than Jonah! . . . There is something here, I tell you, greater than Solomon!' – the king who was the model of wisdom in the Old Testament (Matthew 12:41, 42).

Another saying is preserved in Q (Matthew 13:17) along the same line. Like the saying which we have just mentioned, it may be a tribute paid by the Church to the work of Jesus, or it may be an estimate by Jesus himself of what God was accomplishing through him and his followers. 'Remember this! Many prophets and many of God's people wanted very much to see what you see, but they could not, and to hear what you hear, but they did not.'

5

SALT FOR ALL MANKIND

Christianity has played such an important role in world history, and in so many lives, that it is an important question: *what, if anything, has given this religion its identity?* It is obvious that the Christian religion has changed vastly from century to century, from generation to generation, from denomination to denomination, and even from individual to individual – and it is by no means obvious to everyone what, if anything, is unifying and distinctive about it.

Some variety in Christian outlooks is present within the New Testament. We have already noted some of the differences between the four gospels. There is another immense difference between the letters of Paul, with their constant insistence on faith in God through Jesus Christ, and the letter of James, which scarcely mentions Jesus or faith. And there is a difference between the enthusiasm which excites the Thessalonians or Corinthians to whom Paul writes and the much more orderly and settled atmosphere in the letters to Timothy and Titus. That later atmosphere has been described as 'early Catholicism'. But it is *very* early, *very* undeveloped, and *very* informal, in comparison with the elaborate Catholicism which flourished under the Papacy in the Middle Ages.

Somehow this word 'Christianity' has to be made to cover the Eastern Orthodoxy of the Byzantine empire centred on Constantinople and of the Tsarist empire centred on Moscow – together with the Protestantism of Martin Luther and the Reformed religion of John Calvin in the sixteenth century. Somehow 'Christianity' includes *both* the Pilgrim Fathers crossing the Atlantic and the State Churches from which they were escaping. It also includes *both* the theology of a sophisticated intellectual in Germany *and* the belief of an old peasant woman in Spain; *both* the congregation in a church on Wall Street in twentieth-century New York *and* the little gatherings in an African village; *both* secret prayers in a prison camp under Hitler or Stalin *and* hymns in the freedom of an Australian outstation; both Evensong in an Anglican cathedral *and* Pontifical Mass in St Peter's; *both* the austere worship of strict Protestants *and* an exuberant Pentecostal meeting.

One of the ironies of history is that the essence of the religion named after him has often been thought to lie in something which Jesus Christ hotly rejected. For example, Christianity has often been regarded as a tool of the State and as opium to keep the poor quiet. The irony that such a religion used the name of a homeless man who was crucified needs no emphasis.

Christianity has spent much of its history under the severe control of professional priests and preachers. In practical terms it has looked as if the first duty of Christians was to obey and finance the clergy set over them. We need not deny that some full-time officers have been necessary in the Church – and have been its devoted servants. But we recall that the historical Jesus was very much a layman, with a layman's sense of priorities. He did not live in order to found a society for the support of clergymen.

Pure Christianity has also been identified as a Puritan standard of extra-superior and super-holy behaviour, condemning and where possible censoring the cakes and ale of the ordinary man's appetite. All we need say is that although his followers have always been called to be holy, the historical Jesus was a severe critic of the Pharisees and a table-companion of the outcasts. One thing he was not was 'respectable'.

Modern advocates of Christianity have often identified it as a kind of poetry in praise of things which modern people hold dear anyway – the freedom to elect one's rulers, or the freedom to acquire material goods, or the freedom to express liberal opinions, or the freedom to live one's own life as one's own master. We need not deny that Jesus Christ liberates. But actually he himself managed to live in a colony, with no possessions other than his robe, with few opportunities of the sort that are advertised nowadays; and the freedom he knew and offered came through a life of complete self-sacrifice to God.

Although the word 'Christianity' has been stretched to cover these and many other corruptions, the New Testament makes plain Jesus Christ's rejection of all such perversions of his message. Positively, it affirms 'the Good News' – and if we can discover what the Good News is, we shall be nearer to finding the Christianity of Christ. What, then, is it?

Many modern theologians (following C. H. Dodd) have written about the 'proclamation' (in Greek: *kerugma*) which is to be found in the Acts of the Apostles and elsewhere in the New Testament, and they have argued that here was the original thrust of Christianity. This is an attractive line of investigation, for such theologians rightly emphasize that the New Testament aims to tell good *news*, not to offer good *advice* (at least, not until after the news has been believed and absorbed). But the trouble is that these theologians have summed up the Good News in such a way that it would not convert a fly. According to them, the Good News consisted of an announcement that the suffering Messiah foretold in the Old Testament had appeared in the person of Jesus of Nazareth, who had been raised from the dead to be the judge of all men and the saviour of those who accepted the Good News and were baptized.

Certainly that does sum up several sermons in Acts and elsewhere. But the questions must come thick and fast. What kind of a man was this Jesus? What did he say? What did he do? Why did he suffer? In what way was he the Messiah of Israel? From non-Jews additional questions would be: why should I care whether or not he was the Messiah, and why should I be interested in the Old Testament?

These are not only the questions of the twentieth century. They are questions which Gentiles, and even Jews, would ask face to face with Peter and Paul. It is clear that the life-blood of Christianity must always have been in the personal appeal of Jesus Christ, for it is impossible to be interested in the 'Good News' brought by Christianity unless one has first become interested in Jesus Christ.

What, then, does it mean to be gripped by the news and the appeal of Jesus Christ himself? Plainly it means more than an emotional attraction or an intellectual agreement. John's gospel teaches spiritual truth when it gives the warning of Jesus to Nicodemus who 'one night' went to him with inquiries: 'You must all be born again' (3:7). The heretical Gospel of Thomas attributes to Jesus the saying (also quoted by the great Christian scholar Origen in the first half of the third century): 'He who is near me is near the fire . . .' The outcome of a real meeting with Jesus Christ is shown by Paul to the Galatians: 'I have been put to death with Christ on his cross, so that it is no longer I who live, but it is Christ who lives in me. This life that I live now, I live by faith in the Son of God, who loved me and gave his life for me' (2:19, 20). 'See what big letters I make as I write to you now with my own hand! . . . I will boast only of the cross of our Lord Jesus Christ; for by means of his cross, the world is dead to me, and I am dead to the world' (6:11, 14). Towards the end of his life, Paul asks the Philippians: 'For what is life? To me, it is Christ' (1:21).

If the encounter which has provoked such words is more than emotional or intellectual, it is also more than historical. The Jesus Christ who alone is the life-blood of Christianity is not a figure of the past surrounded by problems, to be congratulated on his strengths and criticized for his limitations. In his second letter to the Corinthians, Paul makes it clear that only a Christ who is more than that can do what Christ has done to him – and to his readers. 'If at one time we judged Christ according to human standards, we no longer do so. When anyone is joined to Christ he is a new being; the old is gone, the new has come' (5:16, 17). To achieve this revolution Jesus Christ has stepped out of the dead past, as Paul indicates in the same letter: 'When [Christ] deals with you he is not weak . . . even though it was in weakness that he was put to death on the cross, it is by God's power that he lives' (13:3, 4). The Good News preached by Paul to the Romans is that Jesus Christ was 'shown with great power to be the Son of God by being raised from death' (1:4).

In John's gospel, we read the promise: 'Because I live you also will live' (14:19). Whether or not those words were spoken by the historical Jesus, they reflect this experience which is the essence of Christianity: *the Christian experience of the contemporary Christ*. And they sum up what matters most in the New Testament's accounts of the meetings with Jesus after his death.

The earliest of these accounts is included in the First Letter to the Corinthians. Paul writes: 'I passed on to you what I received, which is of the greatest importance: that Christ died for our sins, as written in the Scriptures; that he was buried, and was raised to life on the third day, as written in the Scriptures; that he appeared to Peter, and then to all twelve apostles. Then he appeared to more than five hundred of his followers at once, most of whom are still alive, although some have died. Then he appeared to James, and then to all the apostles. Last of all he appeared also to me . . .' (15:3-8).

The importance of this 'Good News' is shown when Paul protests: 'If Christ has not been raised from death, then we have nothing to preach and you have nothing to believe. More than that, we are shown to be lying against God . . . Your faith is a delusion and you are still lost in your sins . . . We deserve more pity than anyone else in all the world' (15:14-19).

But what are we to make of this claim that Christ is 'risen'?

If our own experience corresponds at all deeply with the New Testament's message that a man can be joined to the living Christ and become a new being by becoming a friend of God, and if we have the insight to contrast that message with the despair of the first disciples when Jesus had been publicly tortured to death, we cannot doubt that *something happened* to change those Christians from despair to a radiant and infectious faith. And probably most of us Christians would feel that this is all we need to be certain about, if we are to be Christians ourselves.

Unfortunately we cannot know exactly what happened. Paul's evidence, for example, may refer to an experience which nowadays we should call a psychic experience of someone else's survival of physical death. According to the Acts of the Apostles Paul saw no body when the risen Jesus appeared to him on the road to Damascus, and his own words bear this out. This First Letter to the Corinthians refers to the 'spiritual body' which Christians are to expect after the resurrection of Christ as being as different from the 'physical body' as the plant is different from the seed (seeds were then thought to die in the earth), as the flesh of men is different from the flesh of fish, and as the stars are different from the earth, and Paul says: 'what is made of flesh and blood cannot share in God's Kingdom, and what is mortal cannot possess immortality' (15:35-51). All this tells against a physical resurrection of Christ.

On the other hand, Paul says that Christ 'was buried, and was raised to life on the third day', which seems to imply that the body which had been buried was raised. Also Paul states that his own encounter with the risen but invisible Jesus was extraordinary; he uses a Greek phrase which Today's English Version translates as 'I am like one who was born in a most unusual way.' The New English Bible puts it: 'it was like an abnormal birth.' And we know from (for example) his letter to the Romans that Paul was closer to the belief of the Pharisees in a physical resurrection of the dead than to the Greek idea of the immortality of the soul. 'If Christ lives in you, although your bodies are going to die because of sin, yet the Spirit is life for you because you have been put right with God. If the Spirit of God, who raised Jesus

from death, lives in you, then he who raised Christ from
death will also give life to your mortal bodies by the
presence of his Spirit in you' (8:10, 11).

The conclusion seems to be that to Paul the resurrection of Jesus was not what we should call a
'physical' event. Nor was it what we should call a
'psychic' event. It was the beginning of the new creation,
transcending all present categories. This may be seen in
what Paul writes to the Philippians: 'We are ... citizens
of heaven, and we eagerly wait for our Saviour to come
from heaven, the Lord Jesus Christ. He will change our
weak mortal bodies and make them like his own
glorious body, using that power by which he is able to
bring all things under his rule' (3:20, 21).

The four gospels give more detailed accounts, but
still do not show us exactly what happened. They
do not describe the appearances to Peter and to James
listed by Paul (apart from Luke's bare 'He has appeared
to Simon!' at 24:34). Nor do they describe an appearance to the five hundred. All of the appearances which
Luke recounts took place in Jerusalem; and all of
them as told by John also in Jerusalem apart from
a final appearance in Galilee. The authentic text of
Mark simply says: 'He is going to Galilee ahead of you'
(16:7). Matthew has it that Jesus 'suddenly met them'
in Jerusalem with the message: 'Peace be with you
. . . Do not be afraid. Go and tell my brothers to
go to Galilee, and there they will see me' (28:9, 10).
By 'my brothers' is meant 'the eleven disciples' (28:16).

The Easter stories given to us by Luke are of
imperishable beauty, but they do not enable us to
pin down this phenomenon. What they convey is 'joy
and wonder' (24:41). The risen Jesus expounds 'all the
Scriptures' to the two disciples during their walk to

Emmaus, yet they did not recognize him. He disappears from their sight, but appears to Peter back in Jerusalem and then to all 'the eleven disciples', before whom he eats 'a piece of cooked fish' to show that he is no ghost.

All four gospels tell us that the tomb of Jesus was found to be empty by Mary Magdalene. The Synoptic gospels say that the mother of James was also present; Mark adds Salome, and Luke adds Joanna. Without the reports of subsequent appearances, this report would not be impressive. Perhaps 'what the women said was nonsense' (Luke 24:11), or perhaps it was not a miracle that emptied the tomb. Even when joined with the stories of the appearances, the story of the empty tomb of Jesus will seem to many modern people a mystery. A report given in all four gospels cannot be dismissed out of hand, but this report is still hard to understand and accept. In our time some Christians regard the empty tomb as the supreme miracle. Others regard it as an optional addition to the more solidly authenticated reports that the disciples had psychic experiences.

Both those who accept and those who question the emptiness of the tomb will agree that it is the fourth gospel that gives the deepest interpretation of the life-changing significance of these experiences. Although much Christian experience has come in the fellowship of a group studying the Scriptures or sharing a meal (as Luke implies in his Emmaus story), the heart of the matter has been the individual at the end of his or her tether being called by name and answering *Rabboni* or 'Teacher!' Although Christians have always been convinced that they have been sent to work in the world, the centre of their conviction has been their own

possession of an inner peace and their own assurance of
the reality of the living Jesus.

The peace and the assurance are offered to all, but
Christians do not expect that the offer will quickly be
accepted by all. The frequent harshness of Christian
experience is summed up in Matthew's gospel. 'The
gate is narrow and the way is hard that leads to life,
and few people find it' (7:14). 'Do not think that I have
come to bring peace to the world; no, I did not come to
bring peace, but a sword. I came to set sons against their
fathers . . .' (10:34-36).

Nor do Christians expect that all their problems will
be solved if they do pass through the narrow gate. They
recall that Jesus never set himself up as the arbiter in
all disputes. Luke tells of the reply: 'Man, who
gave me the right to judge, or to divide the property
between you two?' (12:14) According to the early
Christian tradition, Jesus did not claim to have the
answer to all practical problems. It was not for him to
turn everything into gold – or stones into bread. Mark
reports the sad prophecy: 'You will always have
poor people with you' (14:7). According to the
tradition, Jesus did not even lay down one directive
which would answer all personal problems of conscience. Luke tells us *both* of the would-be follower
who was warned that he would have no place to lie
down and rest (9:58) *and* a little later of Martha
and Mary – such different characters! – in their home
(10:38-42). Luke tells, too, *both* of the man who was
commanded to 'sell all you have and give the money to
the poor (18:22) *and* a little later of the tax collector
whose decision to give only 'half my belongings to the
poor' was described by Jesus as 'salvation' (19:8, 9).

The gospels make it clear that Jesus was faced by

the choice: try to give people all the answers they want, or try to give them the freedom to find their own answers. He chose freedom. The story of the temptation in the desert is the drama of this choice (Matthew 4:1-11; Luke 4:1-13). Jesus is tempted to provide an economic panacea – food for himself and for all the poor: 'order these stones to turn into bread!' He is tempted to silence all religious doubts by a miracle: 'throw yourself down to the ground' from 'the highest point of the temple' – and be rescued by angels. He is tempted to use political power to crush his enemies, as lord over 'all the kingdoms of the world, in all their greatness'. In his solitary struggle Jesus recognizes all these as temptations of the Devil. It is, however, tragically correct to point out that Christians have often disagreed with their Master on this point. For Christians have often acted as if Jesus had accepted all these suggestions as excellent ways of dealing with the masses.

What Christians do have in common is a certain detachment from their jobs, homes, and favourite opinions – a certain serenity amid their economic, intellectual, and political problems, when they glimpse the absolute demand and the inexhaustible offer brought to them with 'the Good News'.

Some of those who heard the historical Jesus glimpsed the demand and the offer when they were challenged to leave everything and follow him. In the early years after the death of Jesus (when, incidentally, the apostles seem to have been reunited with their wives and families) the demand and the offer were expressed in terms of the nearness of the End. Thus Paul wrote in the First Letter to the Corinthians: 'There is not much time left, and from now on married men should live as though they were not married; those who weep, as

though they were not sad; those who laugh, as though
they were not happy; those who buy, as though they
did not own what they bought; those who deal in
worldly goods, as though they were not fully occupied
with them' (7:29-31). When most Christians no longer
reckoned the End to be near in time, what marked
Christianity was still the end of any anxious absorption
in the passing show. 'The world and everything in it
that men desire is passing away,' says the First Letter of
John; 'but he who does what God wants lives forever'
(2:17). Always that has been the Christian spirit.
Those who have thought at first that Jesus was a
defeated teacher and a vanished corpse, and who have
then heard his living call and known him as *Rabboni*,
cannot get really interested in anything else.

The teaching of Jesus contained no moral system,
although no doubt a certain amount of systematic
ethical thought became inevitable. Modern 'situation
ethics' – the emphasis that a moral decision is meaning-
ful only when made within a definite situation to make
that situation more loving – is in accordance with the
rebellion of Jesus against the legalism of the religion
around him. But the challenge of Jesus was at the
beginning, and has remained through nineteen centuries,
far more costly than what is normally implied by the
word 'love'. It has been the challenge to love *as he has
loved* – something that people have not grasped until
they have reckoned with the fact that the love in Jesus
drove him to his death.

Always the follower of Jesus has had to undergo a
kind of death, repeated in each new situation of
life. Luke had the insight to call this the 'daily' cross
(9:23, changing Mark 8:34). This has meant the
death of crude selfishness; the more costly death of
self-protection; and the even more difficult (and con-

sequently even rarer) death of self-concern, whether self-approval or self-condemnation. It has meant putting the ego on the cross, while all around the world has whispered and shouted that the only sensible course is to look after oneself, enjoy oneself, and assert oneself before one dies. But those who have managed this real-life following of Jesus always possess something beyond the thousand and one difficulties. They have found life.

The pattern of personal discipleship has thus never altered, although the situations where it has been lived out have been almost infinitely different. There has been the death of self, and the birth of love. There has been the daily cross, and the daily Easter. Of course Christians, like others, do in a sense love themselves – they need to discover themselves (often it takes solitude), to be themselves (often that means being unfashionable). But in a way all their own, the followers of Jesus *are* themselves when they give themselves away. 'I tell you the truth: a grain of wheat remains no more than a single grain unless it is dropped into the ground and dies. If it does die, then it produces many grains.' All Christian life is a commentary on those words in the fourth gospel (12:24).

The teaching of Jesus contained no plan for the Church as an institution, although no doubt a certain amount of organization became inevitable. The stripping down of the institutional Church during the twentieth century is, in many of its features, a return to the original teaching. For churches as for individuals, the wisdom of life as Jesus sees it is immensely simple: 'Whoever wants to save his own life will lose it; but whoever loses his life for me and the gospel will save it' (Mark 8:35). But those who have responded to the challenge of Jesus have always been distinct from the mass of humanity. They have had to be, in order to contribute their distinctive message through their lives. Matthew's gospel puts clearly the function of Christians in the world: 'You are like salt for all mankind' (5 : 13).

6

GOD AND MAN

We have seen how inevitably Christianity has been a religion about Christ when it has been really alive. It has been alive with his unending life. But the name 'Jesus Christ' is not merely a label stuck to a figure created by our own emotions or imaginations – to a parcel of fashionable opinions (religious or secular) which we have picked up from some book or conversation. The name refers to a teacher who had some strong opinions of his own. In Christianity Jesus Christ is proclaimed, but that means proclaiming the heart of what he himself proclaimed. The Revelation to John rightly speaks of 'an eternal message of Good News to announce to the peoples of the earth, to every race, tribe, language, and nation' (14:6).

This Good News, because it is the announcement about Jesus, is also a message about God and man. Jesus expressed this message in a style natural to a Palestinian Jew of the first century, but its essence can be re-expressed in a style natural to later ages including our own. And surprisingly little re-expression is needed if we concentrate on the radiance of the central affirmations. What is needed much more, by many non-Christians and Christians alike, is enough humility to appreciate how permanent the essential message is. The opinions of two Jewish scholars are important and instructive here. At the end of his great study of *Jesus of Nazareth* published in Hebrew in 1923 and in English in 1925, Dr Joseph Klausner wrote: 'In his ethical code there is a sublimity, distinctiveness, and originality in form unparalleled in any other Hebrew ethical code; neither is there any parallel to the remarkable art of his parables.' Almost at the end of his *Jesus the Jew* (1973), Dr Geza Vermes wrote: 'Second to none in profundity of insight and grandeur of character, he is in particular an unsurpassed master of the art of laying bare the inmost core of spiritual truth and of bringing every issue back to the essence of religion, the existential relationship of man and man, and man and God.'

Probably the historical Jesus never met an atheist. Nowhere in his teaching do we find an argument for the existence of God. No such argument was needed in his day – at least not among Jews in Palestine. But in a time such as the twentieth century, when the reality of God is very widely questioned or denied, it is important to note carefully what Jesus meant by God. That will help us to a more vivid sense of the presence of God in life – something more valuable than any 'proof' of God's existence addressed to the intellect alone. And it will also help us by showing that some of the points made by modern atheists were made by Jesus too.

Jesus accepted the basic teaching of the Old Testament about God. That was to be expected, and there is no good reason to doubt the authenticity of those parts of the gospels which emphasize this and keep much of the Jewish phraseology. God is 'Lord of heaven and earth', and the earth is 'the resting place for his feet' (Matthew 11:25; 5:35). 'In the beginning, at the time of creation, it was said, "God made them male and female"' (Mark 10:6). It has often been suggested that this simple faith in God the Creator was encouraged by the beauty of Galilee around the boyhood of Jesus.

We can accept this suggestion only if we also remember that Jesus shows the realism of one brought up close to nature. The wild flowers are more beautiful than Solomon's royal robes – but the point made is practical: 'why worry about clothes?' The grass is clothed by God – but it is 'here today, gone tomorrow'. The sparrows are loved by God – but they fall to the ground dead (Matthew 6:28-30; 10:29). Jesus was no nature-worshipper, and no romantic. To him as to all Jews, the decisive revelation of God's love was in God's dealings with people who are worth more than many sparrows – with Abraham, Isaac, and Jacob (Mark 12:18-27). Jesus knew perfectly well that while nature puts man's petty anxieties in a proper perspective it does very little to answer man's yearnings.

Jesus practised, and insisted on, reverence to God – as did all the tradition of Jewish piety. 'May your holy name be honoured!' (Matthew 6:9) A Q passage tells the disciples to 'be afraid of God, who can destroy both body and soul in hell' (Matthew 10:28). To modern readers one of the most surprisingly fervent sections of the Sermon on the Mount is the teaching about vows. It seems that Jesus had a horror of swearing by anything to do with God (Matthew 5:33-37). So much for the Jewish charge that he was a blasphemer! And so much for the frequent Christian assumption that God is a pal to be taken lightly! But of course this reverence in thought and speech was not the only consequence of the vision of the holy God. God must be honoured in life. 'You cannot serve both God and money'; 'you must be perfect – just as your Father in heaven is perfect' (Matthew 6:24; 5:48). Since this is the standard set before men, the only sensible prayer is: 'God, have pity on me, a sinner!' (Luke 18:13) For a sinner is in a worse position than a man drowned in the sea, or maimed (Mark 9:42-48).

Jesus was well aware of a man's need to wrestle with God in prayer, like Jacob in the Old Testament. The evidence about Jesus shows that he himself reached such a mature confidence in God's goodness that he could say that the obvious injustice of nature was itself a sign of this goodness to all: 'Your Father in heaven makes his sun to shine on bad and good people alike' (Matthew 5:45). But this was no easy optimism. The evidence hints that this was a faith reached after searching prayer – regularly in synagogues and 'lonely places', and if need be for whole nights (Luke 5:16; 6:12).

Two prayers of Jesus which almost all scholars accept as authentic are preserved in the Synoptic gospels, in addition to the Lord's Prayer given to the disciples and the prayer or prayers on the cross. Both prayers throw great lights on the mind of Jesus. The first is a prayer of thanksgiving: 'I thank you because you have shown to the unlearned what you have hidden from the wise . . . by your own choice and pleasure' (Matthew 11:25, 26). The second is a prayer of self-dedication: 'All things are possible for you. Take this cup away from me. But not what I want, but what you want' (Mark 14:36). But the prayers of Jesus are also said to have included intercessions: 'I have prayed for you, Simon, that your faith will not fail' (Luke 22:32).

According to the early Christian tradition, four points were made by Jesus with great emphasis about the right style in prayer. Even many Christians think them unexpected points, and so far as we know they were not often found in the teaching of the first-century rabbis. They seem to give us the authentic voice of this Master of Prayer. There is the insistence on privacy: 'when you pray, go to your room and close the door . . .' This is all the more striking because the only private room in the average Palestinian house was the larder. There is the layman's insistence on a sincere brevity: 'do not use a lot of meaningless words.' There is the insistence on a confident perseverance: 'ask, seek, knock' (Matthew 6:5-7). The follower of Jesus who prays is to be like the widow with grievances wearing down the careless judge – and what an astonishing comparison that is! (Luke 18:1-8) And there is the startling insistence on intimacy.

Calling God *Abba*, 'Father, my Father', in prayer was very unusual indeed among Jews of the first century. Yet Jesus used this word himself and told his disciples to do the same (Luke 11:2). The term comes three times in Q, once in M and twice in L, as well as nine times in John's gospel. One of the leading modern experts on first-century Judaism, Dr Joachim Jeremias, says that he has never come across a similar instance, and no scholar has faulted him. Referring to God as 'our Father in heaven' *was* frequent; what was unusual about *Abba* was the intimacy of using the everyday word of children and the home. It so struck Paul that in his surviving letters he quotes it twice. To the Galatians he writes: 'To show that you are his sons, God sent the Spirit of his Son into our hearts, the Spirit who cries, "Father, my Father!"' (4:6) To the Romans he writes: 'The Spirit that God has given you does not make you a slave and cause you to be afraid; instead, the Spirit makes you God's sons, and by the Spirit's power we cry to God, "Father, my Father!"' (8:15)

This homely word is the key to the novelty in what

Jesus taught about God and man. It shows that the novelty lay not so much in what Jesus said about God as in what he said *to* God – and in how he lived, and taught others to live, towards God. According to Jesus, God is in himself not essentially different from what the Old Testament taught and what the Jews of the first century believed. The difference lies in a new understanding of how God treats men and asks them to treat him. The God of the New Testament runs to man in love, and asks to be loved; the 'Lord of heaven and earth' is *Abba*. What Jesus brings is a new relationship based on a new agreement (or 'covenant' or 'testament'). That is a matter not of theology but of life.

For when we turn to what Jesus said about man, we see that he had no illusions about human nature. John's gospel is psychologically profound in saying that even the close disciples of Jesus needed more than anything else to be shown the Father (14:8) – and that Jesus knew why men could not see the Father. 'He knew all men well. There was no need for anyone to tell him about men, because he knew what was in their hearts' (2:24, 25). Around the little circle where the Son of Man revealed the glory of God lay the world of men – and there 'it was night' (13:30).

Mark sums up the grim picture of man to be found in many of the parables and sayings of Jesus: 'From a man's heart come the evil ideas which lead him to do immoral things, to rob, kill, commit adultery, be greedy, and do all sorts of evil things; deceit, indecency, jealousy, slander, pride, and folly – all these evil things come from inside a man and make him unclean' (7:21-23). Even Luke, who on the whole takes a more sunny view of human nature, thinks it possible for a man to be entirely in spiritual darkness (11:34, 35)

– partly because he has found that teaching in the Q material about Jesus (Matthew 6:22, 23). Q also included a warning against underestimating the difficulties of a man's journey from darkness to light. This is the story about the cottage left 'empty, clean, and all fixed up' – only to be occupied by squatters (Matthew 12:43-45). In other words, Jesus insisted that the evil in human nature went so deep that it was not enough to be converted or cleansed. To be saved, a man needed to be filled with a new goodness, a new light.

Jesus treated a person as a unity of body, mind, and soul. Spiritual healing could bring physical health. Although we feel that Mark was far less interested than Luke in psychology or medicine, we can examine his accounts of healings and find there an estimate of what man needs. The will of Jesus in contact with the will of a 'leper' can heal the skin-disease; the forgiveness of his sins can release a paralysed man; trust in what Jesus commands can make a man stretch out a hand believed to be crippled (1-41; 2:5; 3:5). What is happening is that evil is being overcome by a greater force, as a strong man is overcome, tied up, and gagged by a still stronger man who breaks into his house like a bandit in Galilee (3:27). And this greater force gives courage to soul, mind, and body – overcoming evil, tying up sin, gagging the Devil.

Yet it is a misunderstanding of the work of Jesus to regard it as a Christian version of medical science, so preoccupied with healing that it has registered a complete failure if it has failed to restore health. The gospels frequently insist that it was not the purpose of Jesus to heal as many people as he could reach. That is a point made at the beginning of Mark's gospel. One evening 'people brought to Jesus all the sick' and

'Jesus healed many who were sick' – but long before daylight Jesus got up, left the house, and went away to pray and to preach (1:32-39). At the end of Mark's gospel the point recurs. Jesus was a doctor who did not secure his own health, a saviour who by the normal standards of health and success could not save himself (15:31). Mark simply leaves us with the scandal that the God who had given health to many through Jesus apparently abandoned Jesus in his agony (15:34). Somehow that is part of 'the Good News about Jesus Christ, the Son of God' (1:1) – for it makes Jesus the brother of all the defeated.

It is impossible to make sense of the priorities of Jesus without acknowledging that to him the most important fact about a person was his or her relationship with the eternal God. There have been various attempts by modern atheists to extract from the teaching of Jesus some true message about man's freedom, or man's fulfilment in love, or man's capacity to transcend his limitations by dreaming of glory; but if God has to be left out of an account of the message of Jesus it would be more logical and more honest to leave Jesus out too. As a valuable teacher, Jesus stands or falls with the reality of the God he calls 'Father, my Father!'

The inevitability of death looms large in the records of his teaching. As much as any man in any generation, Jesus saw life running towards death. 'Which one of you can live a few more years by worrying about it?' (Matthew 6:27) 'You fool! This very night you will have to give up your life; then who will get all these things you have kept for yourself?' (Luke 12:20) It is clear that Jesus refused to join popular speculations about the conditions of life after death. His austere teaching was that even the institution of marriage would be no more. 'When the dead rise to life they will be like the angels in heaven' – and their rising will depend solely on God's power and love as shown in history (Mark 12:18-27). But Jesus insisted that even after death God the Father would remain 'the God of the living, not of the dead' – and that for this reason 'a man's true life is not made up of the things he owns, no matter how rich he may be' (Luke 12:15). And Jesus placed great emphasis on the idea, already familiar in the teaching of the rabbis of his time, of being rich towards God.

The gospels agree, and emphasize, that Jesus taught that it was possible for an individual to fall out of this eternal relationship with the Father and therefore out of eternal life. Naturally he used the imagery of his people and his time to describe eternal death – the jail for punishment (Matthew 18:34-35), the fire in Hades separated by a deep pit from the feast at Abraham's side (Luke 16:22-24), the smouldering fire and the maggots of the rubbish dump in the Valley of Hinnom outside Jerusalem (Mark 9:48). But again and again he said or implied that such a separation from life and blessedness was contrary to the will of God and contrary to the true nature of man.

Jesus was a humanist who believed that, however foolish, rebellious and estranged he might be, man remained God's son, a creature with a unique dignity. All religious discipline was therefore 'for the good of man', not the other way round (Mark 2:27). And the love which Jesus showed to humanity was not merely theoretical. He loved people one by one and noticed what they actually needed. He knew that an unskilled, unemployed labourer desperately needed a *denarius* a day – the silver coin which was reckoned the minimum on which a man could keep a family (Matthew

20:1-15). He knew that a wife would go frantic if she had mislaid one of the ten silver coins making up the headdress which was her dowry (Luke 15:8-10). The world where he lived was not the world of ideas, or the world of politics. As is shown so often by the stories he told, it was the world of fields, kitchens, and markets. It was a world where strangers needed hospitality, not a vague blessing (Matthew 25:35), even if a man was already in bed with his children around him – and his family had eaten up all the day's baking of bread (Luke 11:5-8).

Essentially what Jesus did to people was to make them believe *for themselves* in God their Father and so *in themselves* as God's children. Typical is the report of his healing of 'a woman who had suffered terribly from severe bleeding for twelve years' – who was drained of fitness and energy, and who according to the custom of the time was reckoned useless, cut off from the fellowship of the village and the friendship of neighbours. Power and peace went from him to her in her obscure humiliation (Mark 5:25-34).

To Jesus, people always could be forgiven, and therefore restored to the dignity that was their proper possession, if only they did not cut themselves off in arrogance. It was only the people who refused to forgive others who could not be forgiven; only the people who refused to humble themselves before God who could never get through to God; only the people who would not take the log out of their eye who could not see even how blind they were (Matthew 7:5); only the people who had so shut themselves off from reality that they described healing as evil who had committed an eternal sin (Mark 3:20-30).

Many parts of the reported teaching of Jesus point to the signs of man's true nature as the son of God. He

was never sentimental. One of the things he admired in
human nature was a sharp eye for what was going on,
such as the redness of the sky at sunset or dawn
(Matthew 16:1-3). He chuckled over the shrewd rogue
who made friends of his master's creditors when he
was about to be dismissed (Luke 16:1-8). But all his
teaching bears out Matthew's summary that Jesus
admired most the pure in heart (5:8). He admired
the humility and trust of children in contrast with the
suspicious pride of 'the men who are considered
rulers' (Mark 9:33; 10:42) – such as 'that fox' Herod
(Luke 13:32). He admired the serenity and determina-
tion of those who trusted life and God. 'Remember this!
If you have faith as big as a mustard seed, you can
say to this hill, "Go from here to there!" and it
will go. You could do anything!' (Matthew 17:20) As
the Sermon on the Mount shows repeatedly, Jesus
admired the merciful – those with the strength to
control their anger and to love their enemies. And he
admired the patient love to be seen in parents. 'As
bad as you are, you know how to give good things to
your children. How much more, then, your Father in
heaven will give good things to those who ask him!'
(Matthew 7:11).

Obviously such teaching about man was presented
without reference to, or awareness of, modern knowledge of man's evolution from other animals and without the benefit of modern psychology, sociology, and so
forth – just as the teaching of Jesus about God made
no reference to modern problems with religious
knowledge and language. It is equally obvious that
if this teaching is going to illuminate modern man, the
simple statements of the first century must be connected
with our complex modern problems. What is not so
obviously true is the continual assertion of modern

atheists and agnostics that the teaching of Jesus has been rendered invalid by modern knowledge and experience. On the contrary, the truth is this: in its central affirmations, the teaching of Jesus presents for ever and to all the littleness and greatness of man, the child of God.

7

THE GOVERNMENT OF GOD

The question of the significance of the teaching of Jesus about the 'Kingdom of God' deserves a chapter to itself, however short the chapter has to be.

If God is as Jesus said he is (allowing for the Jewish poetic form in which Jesus taught), then it follows that God cannot be content with the disorder, the tragedy, and the apparent triumph of evil which are so painfully prominent in human experience and which lead many in modern times to deny God's very existence. So God must show his power. Accordingly the phrase 'the Kingdom of God' or Matthew's equivalent 'the Kingdom of heaven' occurs thirteen times in Mark's gospel, nine times in Q, 27 times in M and twelve times in L. As we have seen (pages 116-19), the phrase means that God is completely acknowledged as King. It was because Jesus claimed that the Kingdom of God was 'near' (Mark 1:15) that he was able to speak about the power of God, and it was because he believed his own teaching that he was able to trust that power. The first Christians confidently believed that 'all these things will happen before the people now living have all died' (Mark 13:30).

Within the period covered by the New Testament, people had to cope with the fact that the Kingdom of God did *not* come as both Jesus and the apostles plainly expected it would. This crisis of faith is reflected in the latest document to be included in the New Testament, the Second Letter from Peter. 'You must understand that in the last days some men will appear whose lives are controlled by their own lusts.

They will make fun of you and say, "He promised to come, didn't he? Where is he? Our fathers have already died, but everything is still the same as it was since the creation of the world!" ' (3:3, 4)

Whoever wrote this letter (after the death of the 'fathers' of the first Christian generation) could still teach: 'Your lives should be holy and dedicated to God, as you wait for the Day of God, and do your best to make it come soon – the Day when the heavens will burn up and be destroyed, and the heavenly bodies will be melted by the heat. But we wait for what God has promised: new heavens and a new earth, where righteousness will be at home' (3:11-13). However, as century has followed century, and the Kingdom of God has still not come, many Christians have given up waiting. The whole world-view of the first Christians seems to many in our time very remote indeed, and in no way does it seem stranger than in this emphasis on waiting for a Kingdom believed to be 'near'.

As there has been an ever more frank discussion of the psychological differences between ancient and modern expectations for the future of the earth, many Christians as well as many sceptics have openly wondered whether the teaching about God and man given by Jesus and his apostles has any relevance. In *Christianity as Old as Creation* Matthew Tindal pleaded for a religion freed from the limitations and mistakes of the first Christian century. As he wrote: 'If they thought their times were the last, no direction they gave could be intended to reach further than their own times.' Those words date from 1730.

At the end of *The Quest of the Historical Jesus*, Albert Schweitzer frankly declared that the teaching of the historical Jesus should not (indeed, *could* not) be accepted by modern men, for this teaching was

thoroughly 'eschatological'. By this Schweitzer meant
that Jesus based everything on the End being near in
time. In later books Schweitzer arrived at his own
alternative to this teaching – the idea of 'reverence for
life', accompanied by a compassion for all suffering life
and a refusal to attempt any philosophical explanation
of why there was the suffering. Schweitzer wrote at the
end of *The Quest*: 'It is not Jesus as historically
known, but Jesus as spiritually arisen within men,
who is significant for our time and can help it. Not the
historical Jesus, but the spirit which goes forth from
him and in the spirits of men strives for new influence
and rule, is that which overcomes the world.' On the
one hand, Schweitzer declares that the historical Jesus
is dead and remote. 'It is not given to history to
disengage that which is abiding and eternal in the
being of Jesus from the historical forms in which it
worked itself, and to introduce it into our world as
a living influence . . . As a water-plant is beautiful
so long as it is growing in the water, but once torn from
its roots withers and becomes unrecognizable, so it is
with the historical Jesus when he is wrenched loose
from the soil of eschatology.' On the other hand,
Schweitzer follows a Jesus divorced from this historical
message. 'The abiding and eternal in Jesus is absolutely independent of historical knowledge and can
only be understood by contact with his spirit which is
still at work in the world.'

How are we to reply to this challenge? Is the message
of Jesus about the Kingdom of God hopelessly out-
dated?

Surely part of the right answer is that as a matter
of history a great crisis *was* 'near' the generation which
the historical Jesus addressed. Some of those hearing

F

him were to crucify him; others were to lead the Christian Church into the world with an amazing assurance. And it was in fact the last generation before the destruction of Jerusalem and the attendant horrors. No man has ever spoken at an hour more critical for his hearers. And to those who responded, a new government emerged which could never be shaken – the government described in the Letter to the Colossians: '[God] rescued us from the power of darkness and brought us safe into the kingdom of his dear Son, by whom we are set free' (1 : 13).

But that is not the whole answer. The promise of the Kingdom of God was not completely fulfilled in the events of the first century. Remembering what had been promised, the early Christians rightly regarded the staggering events which had taken place in their time as no more than the beginning of the 'Day of Christ' to which they still looked forward. At almost the last moment in the Revelation to John a new title is given to Jesus : 'the bright morning star' (22 : 16). Writing to the Romans, Paul gives a sublime expression to the sense that it is barely dawn, not high noon. 'We know that up to the present time all of creation groans with pain like the pain of childbirth. But not just creation alone; we who have the Spirit as the first of God's gifts, we also groan within ourselves as we wait for God to make us his sons and set our whole being free' (8 : 22, 23).

The challenge to us comes in that passionate prayer which ends the Revelation to John (22 : 17, 20): 'The Spirit and the Bride say, "Come!" Everyone who hears this must also say, "Come!" . . . He says, "Certainly so! I am coming soon!" So be it. Come, Lord Jesus!' And at the end of his first letter to Corinth, Paul offers the same prayer – not in Greek but in Aramaic, the

language of Jesus and of the very first Christians:
'*Marana tha* – Our Lord, come!' (16:22) What are we
to make of that prayer which so clearly echoes the
belief of the historical Jesus that the Kingdom of God
would come quickly?

We have seen that the life-blood of Christianity has
been the Christian experience of the contemporary
Christ; and in the next chapter we shall look at some of
the ways in which it is true that, as Schweitzer wrote, the
contemporary Christ 'comes to us as one unknown,
without a name, as of old, by the lake-side, he came to
those men who knew him not.' But it is surely not
necessary to dismiss all the teaching of the historical
Jesus on the ground that the central idea of the future
Kingdom of God is utterly strange and irrelevant to us.

It is relevant partly because of its strangeness from
many modern ways of thinking. It is a *total* world-view.
Modern knowledge is acquired by specializing in
some narrow subject; and modern art or fiction or
drama depicts only one person or one thing in relation
with a few other persons or things. Here is a vision of
life as a whole, with a strange power to haunt, goad,
tease, provoke, enlarge, and inspire. In other words, this
idea of the Kingdom of God discharges one of the
great functions of religion. It disturbs us.

Schweitzer himself saw something of another of the
ways in which the idea is relevant. At first sight it may
seem that any idea that this world as we know it is
about to come to an end makes no sense when uprooted
from what Schweitzer called the 'eschatological soil' of
the first Christian century. But the idea does teach a
detachment from the familiar things of this world, and
it brings a promise to the individual which does not
depend on any of these things. Schweitzer wrote at the
beginning of the twentieth century: 'The very strange-

ness and unconditionedness in which he stands before us makes it easier for individuals to find their own personal standpoint in regard to him . . . That which is eternal in the words of Jesus is due to the very fact that they are based on an eschatological world-view . . . They are appropriate . . . to any world, for in every world they raise the man who dares to meet their challenge . . .' Since Schweitzer wrote, many of the things familiar to him in Europe in 1906 have vanished, yet the essence of Christianity has been shown not to depend on them. The challenge of Jesus to the individual has never been forgotten, and Schweitzer has not been the only person raised to spiritual greatness by responding to that challenge. We may expect that in the future the challenge will sound as imperiously as it ever did, and that many more will be called to the decision which makes Christians.

The idea of the Kingdom of God offers a meaning to the whole of a person's life, for it sets that life in a pattern which has meaning. Two of the gospels express this in their stories of what happened as Jesus was dying – stories which may not be accurate history. Luke says that one of the criminals being crucified with Jesus said to him: 'Remember me, Jesus, when you come as King!' (23:42) It is the only time in the four gospels when anyone calls him 'Jesus', and it voices the faith that a connection with this man and his idea can save a worthless bandit from death's final obliteration. John says that one of the Roman soldiers lifted up to the lips of Jesus a sponge full of cheap wine, thus enabling Jesus to cry in his last extremity: 'It is finished!' (19:29, 30) That soldier, too, finds his place as God's purpose is worked out and its accomplishment is proclaimed.

The Kingdom of God is, however, something bigger

than the individual. It is a social idea, almost a political one; and its natural modern translation is the Government of God. It puts the person in the context of a whole society, acknowledging how deeply the influence of the society shapes the person. In his or her sin the person is corrupted by the society, and if the person is to be liberated from all that is meant by sin there must be a change in the society, so that the crowd gathered to do evil becomes the family assembled for the feast of life and blessedness. Here is the charter for all political struggles which are submitted to the will of God. But here is something better than a challenge to struggle. Here is the promise of victory. Human nature is such that there can be no struggle without the energy given by hope. The idea that ultimately God will take over the government provides the least fragile kind of hope.

As expressed in the New Testament, the idea may seem nonsense because it involves changes in nature to surround the changes in history. Jesus and the first Christians were restrained in comparison with others of their time who prophesied natural calamities to be followed by a supernatural affluence on earth. But the link between history and nature is present in the New Testament. And perhaps our own generation is better placed than most to see the meaning of it. Are we not concerned about the pollution and exhaustion of the earth's resources because of man's folly? Are we not aware of the ruin and poison that can be spread by modern weapons of war? Do we not glimpse the plenty there could be if man would be wise?

This idea of the Kingdom of God is not a prediction of inevitable progress – a promise that there will be no cruel pains or harsh tests. On the contrary, firmly near the centre of all that the New Testament says about the future is the prophecy of tragedy. But the New Testament adds that the tragedy is itself overcome by the continuing purpose of God. Thus in Mark's gospel (13:8), we read: 'Countries will fight each other, kingdoms will attack one another. There will be earthquakes everywhere, and there will be famines. These things are like the first pains of childbirth.' And in Matthew's version of the Lord's Prayer we are asked to say: 'Do not bring us to hard testing, but keep us safe from the Evil One' (6:13).

There is also no complete commitment to the hope that the End will come soon. We have seen that Jesus disclaimed knowledge of the date (pages 122-4). That was what enabled the early Christians to survive the disappointment of their hopes. Often in Christian history the expectancy has revived, only to slacken again. In the long periods when there has been no exciting vision, Christians have been able to console themselves with the parables of Jesus about the seed growing secretly and slowly, including many weeds and thorns, some of it in shallow soil under a scorching sun. Originally those parables were, it seems, told about the preparation in the history of Israel and in the life-time of Jesus for the arrival of the Kingdom of God; but their spiritual meaning is strong for any age. There are many signs in the gospels that the Christians in the second half of the first century adjusted their telling of the parables in order to address their own circumstances and answer their own problems – which included the growing problem of the delay in the promised Kingdom. It was not wrong for those Christians to meditate on the teaching of the historical Jesus and apply it in this way. No, it is for every generation to do the same.

Many modern people ask why it was within the purpose of God that Jesus of Nazareth should hope

for the quick coming of the Kingdom. Why was his
vision so intense that his Father's will would soon be
done in the towns and villages of Galilee and Judea as
in heaven? Why did he teach his followers to hope with
a similar passion, even if it meant being punished by a
disappointment as bitter as his own? Surely the answer is
that he was a man. In order to be human he had to
belong to some group whose world-view he would
accept in parts and reject in parts, according to his
education and experience – and the group where he
lived was the Jewish, and in particular the Galilean,
people at a time when hopes of the coming Kingdom
were many. And we may guess that, even had he
been born into a less expectant community, a man with
such a vision of God would always experience in the
depths of his soul the hope that in his time this
loving Father would triumph. To him, belief in God
would be no comfortable convention but a light in
darkness. He would always hope that the light would
soon shine fully on him and on all men. Because the
earth – made so lovely by God – had been so thoroughly
polluted by the crimes and follies of mankind, he
would always wish to set it on fire.

8

WHO DO YOU SAY I AM?

A turning point in the Synoptic gospels comes when Jesus takes his disciples to the area north of Galilee, under the snow-covered Mount Hermon. There he asks these followers of his: 'Tell me, who do people say I am?' They report various popular attitudes. He is John the Baptist risen from the dead; he is Elijah, come back; he is one of the prophets.

Then Jesus presses them. 'What about you? *Who do you say I am?*' (Mark 8:27-29)

It is a question left with every generation and individual confronting Jesus. And it is a question which seems to be asked by the very nature of the evidence about Jesus.

We readily see that the popular answers which the disciples reported were too backward-looking or too vague. We see why Peter's reply 'You are the Messiah' was in comparison a breakthrough of insight, enabling Jesus to regard the absolute essentials in the training of his disciples as complete – so that he could begin to prepare them for the journey to his death (Mark 8:29-31). For the *Messiah* (Hebrew) or *Christos* (Greek) – the royal deliverer of Israel, anointed by God – was far more than any figure out of the past; he was the man to inaugurate a new age of freedom and splendour. We see all this. But it is equally important, although harder, to see something else. At that stage Peter understood little of the mind of Jesus. According to the gospels, a few moments later Jesus called him 'Satan'. Neither the title 'Messiah' nor any other title to be found in the New Testament was an entirely adequate response to the challenge of the mystery of Jesus. These titles deserve our careful and respectful study. But they are not so perfect that all we have to do is to respect them.

Many passages in the New Testament show how familiar and precious to all the first generation of Christians were the words 'Jesus Christ' or 'Christ Jesus' or 'Christ'; and it is natural to suppose that the purpose of Jesus was to teach that he was Christ. But our familiarity with 'Messiah' or 'Christ' as a title for Jesus should not blind us to the fact that in the first century it was associated with the visible deliverance of the Jews from foreign rule and all adversity.

The Messiah was to be a descendant of King David, restoring David's Kingdom. This 'Son of David' was to be a rebel, a freedom-fighter, a general, a judge, and an administrator. He was to establish justice in the law courts and prosperity in the markets. It appears from their recently discovered scrolls that the monks of Qumran expected the arrival of a priest who would be the companion and chief of this political and military deliverer – the 'Messiah of Aaron' to be the senior colleague of the 'Messiah of Israel'. But there is no evidence that many Jews went in for such a refinement. The whole concentration was on the thought of the Messiah as the miraculously successful statesman. And so the title was an odd one to use about Jesus of Nazareth, the crucified carpenter, who never got nearer political power than when he stood in front of Pontius Pilate. It was a little like calling a very controversial American preacher 'Mr President'.

Some traces remain in the New Testament of the awareness of this oddity. Peter's sermon on the first Whitsunday, as reconstructed in the Acts of the

Apostles, declares: 'it is this Jesus, whom you nailed to the cross, that God has made Lord and Messiah!' (2:36) A very early Christian prayer, reconstructed in the same book by Luke, refers to Jesus as 'your holy servant, whom you made Messiah' (4:27). These seem to be relics of an early belief that Jesus was not always the Messiah – that God had given him the title after his death, as a reward for his obedience in undergoing such sufferings. This belief seems also to be expressed in the Christian hymn quoted by Paul to the Philippians (see page 40).

We have already seen that a leading theme of Mark's gospel is that Jesus prohibited the use of this title about him (page 60). We have suggested that, if Jesus actually did regard himself as the Messiah, the explanation of any fact to which Mark refers may be that Jesus knew that the open use of the title would bring down the wrath of the Romans (page 90). But it may also be that, at least for most of his lifetime, Jesus refused to agree that the title was appropriate.

In the Synoptic gospels there is a curious reference to Psalm 110. We know from other parts of the New Testament and from elsewhere that this psalm was widely regarded as a prophecy of the triumph of the Messiah. But here, it is questioned. 'How can the teacher of the Law say that the Messiah will be the descendant of David?' The psalm seems to show its author (David) calling the Messiah 'my Lord'. 'How, then, can the Messiah be David's descendant?' (Mark 12:35-37) Whether it was Jesus or a Christian who first got into controversy on the interpretation of this psalm, the passage does seem to show an awareness that the Lord Jesus did not fit easily into the role of Son of David.

Such awareness also seems present in the opening chapters of the gospels. Paul tells the Romans that the

Good News is about Jesus Christ: 'as to his humanity, he was born a descendant of David' (1:3). But Mark tells us nothing about Jesus before his baptism, and then refers to him as 'the carpenter, the son of Mary' (6:3). Matthew (1:1-17) and Luke (3:23-38) do give family records or genealogies, but these are different and we cannot be sure about either their sources or their authenticity. One traces the descent from Joseph's father Jacob to David's son Solomon, and so to Abraham; the other, from Joseph's father Heli to David's son Nathan, and so to Adam. It is clear that the Church had no single, reliable 'family tree' for Jesus. In any case, both Matthew and Luke tell us that Joseph had nothing to do with the conception of Jesus, and they do not explain how their accounts of a virgin birth are related to their genealogies. The descent of Jesus from David is by no means impossible, historically speaking. About a thousand years after David, many Jews must have been able to make a similar claim. But the evidence is not clear.

In the gospels, although Jesus is called 'Son of David' by others there are surprisingly few occasions when he clearly calls himself the Messiah. Even in John's gospel the only occasion is in the talk with the Samaritan woman (4:26). In Luke's gospel the occasion is in the talk with the disciples on the first Easter Day (24:26, 46). In Matthew's gospel the only occasion is indeed placed before the crucifixion, but the saying seems to arise out of the life of the Church after Easter: 'Nor should you be called "Leader," because your one and only leader is the Messiah' (23:10).

In Mark's gospel Jesus answers 'I am' to the solemn question of the High Priest: 'Are you the Messiah, the Son of the Blessed God?' – but he immediately goes on to speak of the 'Son of Man' not the Messiah (14:

61, 62). Matthew gives the reply as: 'So you say' (26:64). Luke gives it as: 'If I tell you, you will not believe me, and if I ask you a question you will not answer' (22:67-68). And when Pilate asks him 'Are you the king of the Jews?' Jesus answers 'So you say' in Mark (15:2), as in Matthew and Luke.

We cannot recover exactly what the historical Jesus would have meant on this occasion by 'So you say'. Usually the phrase seems to have had the tone of politeness without a complete agreement. But in any case we cannot recover exactly what the historical Jesus did say to the High Priest or to Pilate. There were no Christians present. All that we can be sure of is that although Mark, Matthew, and Luke certainly believed that Jesus was the Messiah, they were restrained in saying that he openly claimed to be.

According to them, the title which Jesus preferred for himself was 'Son of Man'. So the phrase deserves our specially careful attention. In the Synoptic gospels the title occurs 69 times; in passages occurring only once in Mark, Matthew, or Luke, 38 times; and in John's gospel thirteen times. The title is always used by Jesus, never about him. The evidence appears decisive that Jesus called himself the 'Son of Man'.

Yet many scholars believe that he did not. This may seem an example merely of the perversity of scholars, but truly there is room for doubt. There are two problems.

One is that the phrase 'a son of man' (*bar nasha*) was then used by the Jews where we should say 'a man' or just 'man'. In particular it was used as a polite way of referring to oneself without saying 'I'. The prophet Ezekiel, for example, often says that God addressed him as 'son of man', and Paul referred to himself in the Second Letter to the Corinthians as 'a certain Christian man' – or, as the Greek had it, 'a man in Christ' (12:2). It is possible that Jesus used this way of speaking about himself. For example, when his critics protested that 'no man can forgive sins; only God can!' Jesus may have replied: 'I will prove to you . . . that a man has authority on earth to forgive sins' (Mark 2:10). When they complained about his disciples' behaviour on the Sabbath, he may have said: 'the Sabbath was made for the good of man . . . so man is lord even of the Sabbath' (Mark 2:27, 28). When a rabbi offered to go with him wherever he went, he may have warned: 'Foxes have holes, and birds have nests, but this man has no place to lie down and rest' (Matthew 8:20, also in Luke). It is possible that the gospel-writers were so used to the title 'Son of Man' for Jesus that they used it in places where Jesus meant only 'I'. For example, Luke has: 'Happy are you when men . . . say that you are evil, because of the Son of Man' (6:22) – although Matthew has: 'Happy are you when men . . . tell all kinds of evil lies against you because you are my followers' (5:11). And Matthew has 'Who do men say the Son of Man is?' (16:13), although Luke has 'Who do the crowds say I am?' (9:18)

Another problem is that 'Son of Man' *as a title* (as we might say: 'The Man') was, so far as we know, always used to refer to a figure expected at the End. He would be historical but also supernatural, human but also superhuman.

The title occurs in 'apocalyptic' writings that have survived, written in the first half of the first century and bearing the names of Enoch and Ezra. It may well have been used in other such writings now lost, and possibly it was on many lips – but we have no evidence how widespread was its use. It is, however, fairly certain that the most prominent use of 'Son of Man' as a title was in a passage in the Old Testament. In the Book of Daniel (7:13) there comes a vision of 'one like a son of man' (New English Bible: 'like a man') who rises with the clouds to 'the Ancient of Days' (New English Bible: 'Ancient in Years') and is given glory and royal power. The vision is explained: the royal power will finally be given to 'the people of the saints of the Most High' – in other words, to the Jews who remain faithful to God the Ancient (7:27). The 'Son of Man' represents Israel triumphant at the End.

It would certainly cause astonishment and bewilderment if a carpenter, teacher, and healer going about among people in a Roman colony, subject to weariness, disappointment, and death, claimed such a title for himself. There is no exact modern equivalent, but it would be a little like a man we met in the street telling us: 'I'm the last man on earth.' Yet the gospels contain no trace of puzzlement resulting from the use of this title by Jesus. The question inevitably arises: did he really use it?

In Mark's gospel we have a quotation from the Book of Daniel in what Jesus says to the High Priest: 'You will all see the Son of Man seated at the right side of the Almighty, and coming with the clouds of heaven!' (14:62) And there are other sayings of Jesus which refer to the Son of Man in his glory at the End. 'If a man is ashamed of me and of my teaching in this godless and wicked way, then the Son of Man will be ashamed of him when he comes in the glory of his Father with the holy angels' (8:38). 'In the days after that time of trouble the sun will grow dark, the moon will no longer shine, the stars will fall from heaven, and the powers in space will be driven from their courses. Then the Son of Man will appear, coming in the clouds with great power and glory' (13:24-25). Many scholars believe that such sayings preserve evidence that Jesus expected either to reappear in the future, or to be vindicated by another who would be the Son of Man. But these scholars conclude that Jesus did *not* claim that he already was the Son of Man.

In Matthew's gospel we read the prediction to the apostles: 'you will not finish your work in all the towns of Israel before the Son of Man comes' (10:23). Later we find a section on the coming of the Son of Man at the End (24:27-44), paralleled in Luke's gospel, where we also find the question: 'Will the Son of Man find faith on earth when he comes?' (18:8) All these passages are puzzling, but many scholars think that they, too, may point to the authentic use of this title by Jesus to describe a *future* appearance.

What we do know is that the first Christian generation believed that Jesus was the Son of Man who would appear as judge at the End – and always had been the Son of Man, even in the days of his humiliation. They shared the vision of Stephen in the Acts of the Apostles: 'I see heaven opened and the Son of Man standing at the right side of God!' (7:56) And gradually they had seen that this glory had always belonged to Jesus, 'the Son of Man, who came down from heaven' (John 3:13). They saw that Jesus the Son of Man was given great glory in the hour of his death (John 12:23), when he was lifted up (John 12:34). They wrote all their gospels in this faith and vision. But their use of the title 'Son of Man' about the historical Jesus continued to puzzle Jews who knew how the title had originated. When in Mark's gospel we read the question, 'Why do the Scriptures say that the Son of Man will suffer much and be rejected?' (9:12), we know that the stock Jewish answer would be that nowhere in the Scriptures could any words be found suggesting any such thing – although certainly the people of God had to suffer *before* the triumph of the Son of Man.

We have seen that these titles 'Messiah' and 'Son of Man' were strange titles to use in describing the actual life of Jesus. That life summed up on the cross bore little relation to the Jewish hopes of a victorious struggle under the Messiah, a struggle which was to lead to the final glory personified in the triumphant Son of Man.

It was also true that neither title was ideal in expressing the Christians' sense of the *present* power of Jesus, invisibly in their midst as they worshipped and invisibly their companion as they walked through life. For the titles 'Messiah' and 'Son of Man' could both be regarded as titles to do with the glorious future. Their use might suggest the absence of Jesus from the present age of struggle and tragedy. This, indeed, is what Peter seems to be teaching in one early sermon reconstructed in the Acts of the Apostles (3:20-21) – where God is present and will send Jesus. Jesus is 'the Messiah he has already chosen for you. He must remain in heaven until the time comes for all things to be made new.'

In this speech in Acts (3:22), Peter applies to Jesus a quotation from Deuteronomy (18:15). 'Moses said, "The Lord your God will send you a prophet, just as he sent me, who will be of your own people. You must listen to everything that he tells you."' The same reference is made in Stephen's speech (7:37). These may well be reflections of an early attitude to Jesus like the attitude which his disciples no doubt had to

John the Baptist. Here was not only one prophet among many, but *the* prophet who was due to announce the end of time. And in the same speech Peter calls Jesus simply God's 'Servant' (3:13, 26). That may well be an echo of the use among the first Christians in Jerusalem and other Jewish cities of the title 'Servant of God', which was taken from chapter 53 and elsewhere in the Book of Isaiah. Matthew twice quotes this Old Testament description of the Servant and applies it to Jesus: 'He himself took our illnesses and carried away our diseases' (8:17) and 'he will not argue or shout ...' (12:15-21).

Some evidence survives of a Christian group called the Ebionites, living through the early centuries in poverty and obscurity in the area of Palestine specially on the East bank of the Jordan. This group denied the virgin birth of Jesus, but their puritanism was so strict that they also denounced the sacrifices in the temple and even cut out the mention of locusts from the diet of John the Baptist, for they were complete vegetarians. The only one of the New Testament gospels that they accepted was Matthew's, suitably edited. Otherwise they had their own accounts of Jesus, now lost apart from fragments. A fairly similar group has been described by some fourth-century Christian writers in their accounts of the sect of the 'Nazarenes' in Syria. It seems probable that such groups had their own theories and legends but essentially formed a kind of fossil, preserving the early attitude that Jesus was *the* Prophet and *the* Servant, filled with God's Spirit at his baptism. This attitude could be held together with a strong Jewish piety and morality (such as we see in the New Testament in the Letter of James – where Jesus is scarcely mentioned). But experience showed most Christians that the titles 'Prophet' and 'Servant' were too modest to account for the revolutionary impact of Jesus. Although we know that Jesus was still being called 'your Servant' in prayers at the turn of the first and second centuries (these prayers are preserved in the First Letter of Clement and the *Didache*), the short creed of the Christians to whom Paul wrote was not 'Jesus is the Prophet' or 'Jesus is the Servant of God' but 'Jesus is Lord.' This was what was said or sung by the Christians in Rome (10:9), Philippi (2:11), Corinth (I Corinthians 12:3), and no doubt elsewhere.

However, even the title 'Lord' (*Kurios*) did not say enough. If Jesus was called 'Lord' before his death, as the gospels say he was, not much more than the modern 'sir' can have been meant. Once in Mark's gospel Jesus sent two of his disciples to get hold of a donkey using the phrase 'the Lord (*Kurios*) needs it' (which may have been a previously arranged pass-word), but Today's English Version is probably correct to translate this: 'The Master needs it' (11:3). Once in John's gospel the apostle Philip is called *Kurios*, translated as 'Sir' (12:21). In the ancient world many gods and many men were called lords.

It was the same with the title 'Son of God'. The Kings of Israel had often been called the sons of God, as the psalms show. In the first century the Jewish rabbis often compared God with a father, which suggested that all men were his sons, and the evidence is that many wonder-workers called themselves 'sons of God'. In the pagan world the use of the title was so widespread that Mark thought it possible that a Roman army officer had exclaimed after witnessing the death of Jesus, 'this man was really the Son of God!' (15:39) – which Matthew repeated but which Luke changed into 'Certainly he was a good man!' (23:47)

All the gospels do their best to show that Jesus was, and is, 'lord' and 'son' in a unique sense. For example, Mark (who certainly means the officer's tribute on Calvary to be understood in a unique sense) reports a parable where many slaves sent by its owner to claim the profits of a vineyard are ejected and eventually 'the man's own dear son' is killed (12:1-12). Everywhere in the gospels Jesus is quoted as talking about 'my Father' *or* 'your Father'. (The 'Our' beginning Matthew's version of the Lord's Prayer, 6:9, is 'how you should pray'.) John's gospel only emphasizes this convention: 'my Father and your Father' (20:17). And the most vivid way of stressing the uniqueness of the sonship of Jesus was found when Matthew and Luke included in their gospels the stories which have made the beauty and devotion of Christmas – the virgin birth, the angels in the sky, the homage of the men from the east.

But the decisive stage in separating Jesus from other lords and other sons was taken outside the Synoptic gospels. This was the stage of saying that Jesus existed before his human conception and birth. We do not know when or how this step was taken. One of the earliest indications that it had been taken (and was already familiar to Christians) comes during Paul's discussion of a collection to aid the poverty-stricken congregation in Jerusalem, in the Second Letter to the Corinthians. 'For you know the grace of our Lord Jesus Christ; rich as he was, he made himself poor for your sake . . .' (8:9).

From that it probably seemed a short step to saying that Christ had been God's agent in the creation of the universe with all its 'sons' and 'lords'. We know that it had become customary for Jews to think of the Wisdom of God as a person who had been God's agent in the creation, and no doubt Christian thought moved in the same direction. In the First Letter to the Corinthians, we read Paul's teaching that 'there is only one Lord, Jesus Christ, through whom all things were created' (8:6). In the Letter to the Hebrews we have another statement that after many prophets 'in these last days God has spoken to us through his Son. He is the one through whom God created the universe . . .' (1:2). And at the beginning of John's gospel, we have the faith proclaimed that the Word who 'became a human being' was 'with God' and 'the same as God' eternally. 'Through him God made all things; not one thing in all creation was made without him.'

However, this too turned out to be an unsatisfactory way of talking about Jesus. Not only did it lose much of its appeal when talk about 'the Word' (in Greek *Logos*) running through the universe ceased to be fashionable in philosophy. It also left unclear the question of the nature of Jesus – as long controversies were to show in the history of the Church. In what way was this unique Son begotten before anyone was created? In what way was this Word the agent of God yet the same as God? Was it right to continue to speak of God *and* him? Were not the Father and the Son equally divine? These were some of the questions left unanswered in the New Testament. And there was another question which probably perplexed more Christians than liked to voice their doubts, and which remained a rooted objection in the minds of Jews and pagans. Was it not nonsense to speak of Jesus having created the universe – as if the stars came from the same hand as the shavings in the Nazareth shop?

Before the New Testament closes, it gives us a few glimpses of the coming decisions by the Catholic Church in its councils beginning at Nicaea (325) – decisions which will insist that God the Son has the same 'substance' as God the Father, and equal glory. The longest glimpse is provided by John's gospel, as we have seen. In the Letter to Titus (2:13) and the Second Letter from Peter (1:1) there are references to Jesus as 'our God and Saviour'. In the Letter to the Hebrews (8:9) a quotation from the Greek version of a psalm (45:6) is addressed by God to Jesus: 'Your throne, O God, will last forever and ever!' But these are no more than glimpses of the theological future. The great dogmatic definition of the person of Christ which the Church adopted at the Council of Chalcedon in 451, after more than a century's debate, belongs to a different age and a different world. The men who wrote the New Testament had not learned to think about Jesus in philosophical terms such as 'substance'; and it was their normal rule to distinguish between 'Jesus' and 'God' – even in the four documents just mentioned.

The incomplete discussion in the New Testament shows that Jesus could fit no formula which the first Christian generation could discover. Words failed them as they struggled to express their vision.

Words always have failed, throughout the history of Christian thought. Ultimately this does not matter, for the Jesus portrayed in the Synoptic gospels always gives the impression of a man not chiefly interested in what others would say about him. The saying recorded by Matthew rings true: 'Not everyone who calls me "Lord, Lord," will enter into the Kingdom of heaven, but only those who do what my Father in heaven wants them to do' (7:21). But the attempt to find words to describe Jesus has continued despite its many failures, and (human nature being what it is) presumably always

will continue. He does not need our compliments, but
we need to get our minds clear. It is greatly to their
credit that so many serious and eager theologians of the
past struggled to find clear answers to the questions
about Christ which pressed upon their intellects, hearts,
and consciences.

There is one legitimate reason why Christians hesitate
when told that new thoughts and words are needed in
modern times when new questions have arisen. It is
the fear that in the process of 'revision' or 'restatement'
Christian thought may move away from the vision
of God in Christ which has inspired Christianity
across the centuries. Understandably Christians fear to
lose or to risk the life-blood of personal devotion and
self-surrender to God in Christ which has kept
Christianity vigorous – and Christian. And looking back
over the attempts at revision or restatement in modern
times, we can see that this fear has sometimes been
justified. Some of the attempts have been casually
superficial, or flippantly unworthy of the task. If these
are the only possibilities open, devout Christians may
well prefer to stick to Nicaea and Chalcedon – to the
old doctrines. But as we look back over many attempts at a modern 'Christology' which have been
serious, sincere, and effective, we find that this better
way *is* open. The splendour of the vision and the
energy of the life can be preserved and strengthened
by being renewed. Christianity can be made modern
without ceasing to be itself. All that is needed is
this: the attempts at revision or restatement should
maintain the witness which Paul and John made in the
first century in two key sentences. In his second
letter to the Corinthians, Paul wrote: 'Our message is
that God was making friends of all men through Christ'
(5:19). And the First Letter of John contains the

verdict on the life of Christ: 'See how much the Father has loved us!' (3:1) On the evidence provided by the first Christian century and by later ages of Christianity, it would seem that if modern attempts at revision or restatement are in keeping with those simple words they do not go far wrong.

If it no longer voices our sense of deliverance to call Jesus 'Messiah' or 'Christ', we need to find a new way of greeting him as the most effective liberator. If the hopes of Ancient Israel no longer move us, we need to find a new way of saying that his message is what our own nation most deeply desires for its true freedom.

If the title 'Son of Man' no longer thrills us as the pledge of a victory, we need to find a new title which will express the belief that in Jesus we glimpse the whole point of man's struggle. The character of Jesus is what humanity ought to mean and will mean. The development of *homo sapiens* cannot be expected to reach a higher summit in the sphere of the spirit. These are some of the beliefs which demand to be celebrated in new language, art, and music about Jesus in a scientific age when the evolutionary setting is generally accepted.

If the creed that 'Jesus is Lord' does not sound right in an age when lords are not taken very seriously, we need to find a new style of speaking about him as the boss, the director, the leader, who disarmingly comes to us as our guest and even as our servant.

If the almost domestic description of Jesus as the 'Son of God' has lost some of its force, we need to find a new language about this man at prayer, at rest, and at work – a description which will bring his force home to us. At prayer he is uniquely intimate with God, with the Source of all that exists or is possible, with the Holy disturber of our consciences, with the Beauty to

which we are almost blind. And this God he addresses as
'Father, my Father!' At rest he remains the finest
embodiment we have ever known of the patience we
see in all God's attitude to the creation – and of the love
which we occasionally stumble across as the clue to
why the creation was ever undertaken. At work he is
uniquely powerful: reaching and saving the least and
the lost, and defeating the worst of evil so that
'nothing in all creation will ever be able to separate us
from the love of God which is ours through Christ
Jesus our Lord' (Romans 8:39).

If we find it difficult to accept the Christmas stories of
Matthew and Luke as down-to-earth history, we need to
find new pictures of what we believe to be the facts: the
ultimate origin of the birth of Jesus lay in the will of
God the Father and not in the will of Joseph – and the
moral splendour of his life was due partly to his mother,
a uniquely privileged and strengthened woman who in
the hidden years of the infancy and boyhood co-operated
with the will of God.

If we find it difficult to think of the personality of
Jesus existing before his birth, we need to find a
new way of talking about the facts: his birth was the
most important part man has ever been shown of
the unchanging, loving purpose of the eternal God
– and his life was, as Paul wrote in his second letter to
Corinth, 'the exact likeness of God' (4:4). What
matters, surely, is that we should see for ourselves, and
bring others to see, God's own nature revealed in this
human life – 'God's glory, shining in the face of Christ'
(4:6). The purpose that runs through the universe is
expressed in this man. We may not be able to understand the Letter to the Hebrews about 'the one through
whom God created the universe' (1:2). But this we can
understand – 'He shines with the brightness of God's

glory; he is the exact likeness of God's own being'
(1:3). So modern minds and hearts can worship Jesus
as the love of the Father, now in flesh appearing.

If it is no longer normal for us to think of 'the Word'
in the universe, we need to find new words for the
mystery which we do experience – that this man is
in himself *the* meaning. He gives meaning to our
lives, and therefore some meaning to the enigmas of
history and nature. Because the light which we see in the
face of Jesus Christ is so full of grace and truth for us,
we can dare to look out on a world of tragedy and
see light. 'The light shines in the darkness and the
darkness has never put it out' (John 1:5).

If the swift adoration of 'my Lord and my God'
and 'our God and Saviour' which ends the New
Testament seems to need expansion, we need to find
new ways of putting the experience that in Jesus the
eternal, infinite, awe-inspiring, and terrifying God comes
near, God to us, God for us, our light and our life.

In modern times many attempts have been made to
find the necessary new ways of talking about the
embodiment of God in Jesus. It is not our task in this
book to assess these attempts, or to try to do better.[1]
Our work is done if we have shown that the historical
Jesus meets modern man, and asks him: 'Tell me, who
do people say I am? What about you? *Who do you
say I am?*'

---

[1] I briefly discussed these matters in three paperbacks: *God's
Cross in Our World* (1963), *What is Real in Christianity?*
(1972), *What Anglicans Believe* (1974).

FOR FURTHER READING

The dates are of the first publication in English. The books by Craveri and Cross enable us to see Jesus through the eyes of critical modern journalists. By contrast, Lord Longford's biography is a conservative portrait by a Roman Catholic layman. Books marked * are more technical.

C. K. Barrett: *Jesus and the Gospel Tradition, 1967
Otto Betz: What Do We Know about Jesus?, 1967
Günther Bornkamm: Jesus of Nazareth, 1960
Rudolf Bultmann: Jesus and the Word, 1934;
   Jesus Christ and Mythology, 1958
Marcello Craveri: The Life of Jesus, 1967
Colin Cross: Who was Jesus?, 1970
Oscar Cullmann: *The Christology of the New Testament
   (revised edition), 1963
Peter De Rosa: Jesus Who Became Christ, 1975
Martin Dibelius: Jesus, 1949
C. H. Dodd: The Parables of the Kingdom (revised
   edition), 1961;
   The Founder of Christianity, 1970
A. O. Dyson: Who Is Jesus Christ?, 1969
C. F. Evans: Resurrection and the New Testament, 1970
R. H. Fuller: *The Foundations of New Testament
   Christology, 1965;
   Interpreting the Miracles, 1966;
   The Formation of the Resurrection Narratives, 1972
F. C. Grant: The Gospels: Their Origin and Their Growth,
   1957
Adolf Holl: Jesus in Bad Company, 1972
E. G. Jay: Son of Man, Son of God, 1965
Joachim Jeremias: *The Parables of Jesus (revised
   edition), 1963;

* *The Eucharistic Words of Jesus* (revised edition), 1966;

* *The Prayers of Jesus*, 1967;

* *Jerusalem in the Time of Jesus*, 1969;

* *New Testament Theology: Volume I: The Proclamation of Jesus*, 1971

L. E. Keck: * *A Future for the Historical Jesus*, 1971

Ernst and Marie-Louise Keller: *Miracles in Dispute*, 1969

Joseph Klausner: * *Jesus of Nazareth*, 1925

John Knox: *The Humanity and Divinity of Christ*, 1967

W. G. Kümmel: * *Promise and Fulfilment: The Eschatological Message of Jesus*, 1957;

* *Introduction to the New Testament* (revised edition), 1975;

* *The New Testament: The History of the Investigation of its Problems*, 1973

Lord Longford: *The Life of Jesus Christ*, 1974

T. W. Manson: *The Teaching of Jesus* (revised edition), 1935;

The Sayings of Jesus, 1937;

Ethics and the Gospel, 1960

Malachi Martin: *Jesus Now*, 1975

C. Leslie Mitton: *Jesus: The Fact behind the Faith*, 1973

C. F. D. Moule: * *The Birth of the New Testament*, 1962;

* *The Phenomenon of the New Testament*, 1967

Stephen Neill: *The Interpretation of the New Testament, 1861-1961*, 1964

Norman Perrin: * *The Kingdom of God in the Teaching of Jesus*, 1963;

* *Rediscovering the Teaching of Jesus*, 1967

Norman Pittenger (editor): *Christ for Us Today*, 1968

H. J. Richards: *The First Christmas: What Really Happened?*, 1973;

The Miracles of Jesus: What Really Happened?, 1975

John A. T. Robinson: *The Human Face of God*, 1973

Albert Schweitzer: *The Quest of the Historical Jesus* (revised edition), 1954

Edward Schweizer: * *Jesus*, 1971

B. H. Streeter: * *The Four Gospels* (revised edition), 1930

Geza Vermes: * *Jesus the Jew*, 1973

R. McL. Wilson (editor): * *New Testament Apocrypha, Volume One: Gospels and Related Writings*, 1963
Paul Winter: * *On the Trial of Jesus*, 1961
Heinz Zahrnt: *The Historical Jesus*, 1963

and the other books in this series (facing title page)

INDEX

THE BIBLE READING FELLOWSHIP

Readers of this commentary may wish to follow a regular pattern of Bible reading, designed to cover the Bible roughly on the basis of a book a month. Suitable Notes (send for details) with helpful exposition and prayers are provided by the Bible Reading Fellowship three times a year (January to April, May to August, September to December), and are available from:

UK
The Bible Reading Fellowship,
St Michael's House,
2 Elizabeth Street,
London SW1W 9RQ.

USA
The Bible Reading Fellowship,
P.O. Box 299, Winter Park,
Florida 32789,
USA.

AUSTRALIA
The Bible Reading Fellowship,
Jamieson House,
Constitution Avenue,
Reid,
Canberra, ACT 2601,
Australia.